JIM LEIGHTON, B.A., Presbyterian College, is Tennis Coach, Wake Forest University and Professional at the Old Town Club, Winston-Salem, North Carolina. He spent twelve years at Presbyterian College as tennis coach, and is now one of the outstanding tennis teaching professionals in the United States. His series of articles on the fundamentals of tennis for *World Tennis Magazine* brought him international recognition.

INSIDE TENNIS:

Techniques of Winning

INSIDE TENNIS:
Techniques of Winning

JIM LEIGHTON

Wake Forest University
Winston-Salem, North Carolina

Contributors

PAULINE BETZ ADDIE

BILL LUFLER

BILL MURPHY

CHET MURPHY

WAYNE SABIN

WELBY VAN HORN

DENNIS VAN DER MEER

PRENTICE-HALL, INC.
Englewood Cliffs, New Jersey

PRENTICE-HALL INTERNATIONAL, INC., LONDON
PRENTICE-HALL OF AUSTRALIA, PTY. LTD., SYDNEY
PRENTICE-HALL OF CANADA, LTD., TORONTO
PRENTICE-HALL OF INDIA PRIVATE LTD., NEW DELHI
PRENTICE-HALL OF JAPAN, INC., TOKYO

13-467530-4
Library of Congress Catalog Card No.: 69-14432
Printed in the United States of America

Current Printing (last digit)
10   9   8   7   6   5   4

For Jeff

Jim Leighton is one of the outstanding teaching professionals in the United States. Through his many years of teaching experience, he has developed a formula for teaching that is both inspiring and sound. A series of articles on the fundamentals of tennis by Mr. Leighton in *World Tennis* Magazine brought him international recognition.

This book, "Inside Tennis," is a superb compendium for both novice and experienced players and teachers. The best tennis brains in the teaching profession have contributed, and the result is a thoughtful and intelligent work. Never before has a book been designed by (and for) knowledgeable teaching professionals in collaboration. In addition, even the most advanced players will find many new and challenging theories in these pages.

GLADYS M. HELDMAN
Publisher and Editor
World Tennis Magazine

FOREWORD

This book describes the development of a tennis player from a beginner to a finished player. It is a cooperative effort by eight teachers whose combined playing and teaching experience totals over two hundred and fifty years; they are Pauline Betz Addie, Bill Lufler, Bill Murphy, Chet Murphy, Wayne Sabin, Welby Van Horn, Dennis Van der Meer, and the author. It has been written in the firm belief that tennis is most effectively learned on levels of play (beginner, intermediate, and advanced), in logical steps of progression; it represents the first collaboration of this subject written in accordance with this belief. Its format enables any tennis player to find something of value suitable for his level of playing. It is written for all types of tennis teachers, and it presents all phases of the game so that any instructor, depending upon his teaching task of the moment, can apply them at any stage.

In the early part of my own career I had the good fortune to work with many outstanding teachers of tennis—including Bill Lufler, the late Vernon Marcum, Welby Van Horn, Johnny Hendrix, Elwood Cooke, and others—and found this broad experience invaluable in providing a base upon which to build my own techniques. It is my hope that this book will, in some measure, serve the same purpose for anyone interested in the game of tennis.

I want to thank my collaborators for their considerable contribution to this book and two others who made it possible—Robert Lassister, Jr., former Vice President and General Counsel, Hanes Corporation, and Mason H. Blandford, Sales Manager, Hanes Sports, both of Winston-Salem, North Carolina. I am grateful, also, to Don Leach and Tony Teachey of Winston-Salem, for their interest and help, and to Frank Jones of the Winston-Salem *Journal-Sentinel* for his sequence shots of the Wake Forest University Tennis Team. Chet Murphy's quotations on checkpoints and cues

PREFACE

are from his article, "Selected Principles of Learning with Implications for Teaching Tennis," which appeared in the *Journal of Health, Physical Education and Recreation*. His comments on hitting into levels first appeared in *World Tennis,* as did Van Horn's Balance Approach, in abbreviated form.

Every book has a "without whom"; this book has two— Dr. William B. Toole, Associate Professor of English at North Carolina State of the University of North Carolina at Raleigh, and my wife, Betty.

The final responsibility for use and placement of the materials in this book is mine.

JIM LEIGHTON

CONTENTS

A Philosophy of Teaching and Playing Tennis

PART

I

Arguments rage in all sports over past and present greats. In tennis the battle line is clearly drawn: it centers on the relative merits of the all-court game of the past and the Big Game of the present. The combatants, too, are easily distinguished: in one corner, the older players, spectators, and coaches who peer nostalgically back at the likes of Riggs, Budge, Tilden, Vines, and Perry; in the other, their younger counterparts who know only the players of the present.

Both camps can be accused of distorted vision. If you have never seen the past greats, it is difficult to know their merits, but any wise old-timer must concede that he tends to glamorize the past. Caution and not dogma would seem to be the keynote for both sides, for two very important reasons: it is impossible to compare the abilities of two great players who have never met, and discussion must inevitably consider the merits of two different styles of play.

Today's tennis players play the game of continual attack—the Big Game. Their trademarks are the big serve, the volley, and speed; their style of play is to attack behind the serve and from anywhere in the court; their home is the net. They treat with complete disdain a once honored tenet—that no player should be caught in No-Man's-Land, the area that extends from the base line to the service line. Even so, modern players did not invent the big serve, the volley, or speed. McLaughlin, Tilden, Vines, Budge, and Stoefen all possessed big serves; as far back as 1898, Malcolm Whiteman was national champion on the strength of his volleying, and Barotra and Richards volleyed as well as many of the top players of today. Nor did modern players invent the axiom that the best defense is a strong offense. Johnny Doeg became national champion in 1930 with only a serve and a volley. At least two past players showed a complete disregard for No-Man's-Land: both R. Norris Williams and Henri Cochet were very much at home in this section of the court. They differed

TENNIS—PAST AND PRESENT 1

from modern players, however, in their use of it—they were baseliners *inside* the base line. Cochet, a player of great agility and lightning reactions, is a particularly good example of this style of play. He believed that the future of the game lay in taking the ball earlier and earlier, hitting it always on the rise to give an opponent less time, to gain speed with less effort, and particularly to open up the angles in an opponent's court. Nor was power missing on the groundstrokes—Johnston, Anderson, and Tilden all had pulverizing forehands, and no one before or since has belted the ball any harder than Vines.

Groundstroke and service power and all forms of attack—all these were present in the past. Primarily, though, the past players were base line rallyers; they used the groundstrokes as defensive and offensive weapons, and the net game as a finishing touch. The emphasis in the all-court game was on sound forehand and backhand strokes that enabled a player to defend ALL areas of his court as well as to attack. Rather than attack behind their serves, all-court players preferred to use them to draw the short ball and *then* attack. They preferred finesse to the use of power on the return of serve. Rather than rush the net from anywhere in court, they preferred to outmaneuver their opponent and then, when he was out of position, finish him off at the net. All the subtleties that can be performed with a tennis racket—the lob, change of pace, variation in spin, drop shots, angle shots—were a standard part of their equipment.

But let no one extoll the virtues of these all-court players to the exclusion of the masterful exponents of the Big Game; let no one take the Big Game lightly. It's an intensely fierce game played by men who treat the serve as a new nuclear weapon, the volley as a one-shot affair that brooks no reply. How the tempo has increased! Power is one of the main ingredients, and the net result is a game of continual pressure. Maybe some of the first-class players of this type of game would tear Tilden to pieces. One theory is that all players of the past who did not play this type of game would have to switch to the Big Game today to compete on an even basis, and that the Tilden of the Big Game would defeat the Tilden of the all-court game. Maybe—and maybe it would be a stalemate, with Tilden the Big Game player and Tilden the all-court player swapping wins, depending on the level of their respective games on any given day. (In the past there were always enough net rushers around to raise the question, "Who would win—the great baseliner, or the great net rusher?")

You will note, however, that we put our Big Game player in a special classification by calling him "masterful" and "first class." Between these players and the players of the past there exists one very important similarity —the *masterful* players of the Big Game *possess the groundstroke equipment to defend as well as attack*. No matter how offensively or defensively a man plays, he must defend every other game. The first-class exponents of the Big Game have developed the groundstrokes to return serve effectively and, of course, to defend from the backcourt when attacked.

The best players of today's game are power merchants *extraordinaire*. Modern tactics must be seriously reckoned with by teacher and player alike; however, no one who has never seen the great all-court champions of the past can afford to scoff when he hears of their exploits, because they made the playing of the game an art. To admire Kramer, Gonzales, and Emerson need not exclude our awe for Tilden, Perry, Budge, and Riggs.

And now that we have relegated the past-and-present argument to rainy-day locker room fun, what is the value of this brief historical view to us as teachers of the game? Are we in the business of developing championship players? Not exclusively, by any means. We also teach groups, college classes, and college teams with pupils of varying abilities and in varying stages of development. We spend many hours with the untalented, and if we are doing the right kind of job, we are as interested in them as in the talented.

What then is the value if we are not running a factory for champions? It is perspective. To see the game whole, to realize fully that tennis, like everything else, is rooted in the past. And to know that lessons of the present can be just as important as lessons of the past. When the merits of past and present players are viewed from the proper perspective, it becomes obvious that the difference between the two games is merely *accent*—obviously, you must possess some kind of groundstrokes, net game, and serve to play the game on any level, but if the accent is on attack through serve and volley, the groundstrokes may suffer from disuse, if indeed they were ever properly developed in the beginning. In modern tennis, concentration on the serve and volley has brought them to high-level skills, but it has left the groundstrokes somewhat atrophied.

What is most noticeable in tennis today is that everyone plays the Big Game on all surfaces (with the exception of the cagey pros). Everyone rushes the net behind services big and small and from anywhere in court that they can get their racket on the ball. And everyone goes for broke on return of serve (too infrequently breaking). Everyone has the same pattern of play. This seems surprising for two reasons: there is a wide range in the possibilities for hitting and playing a tennis ball, and tennis games are tailor-made to individual differences—emotional, physical, and intellectual.

In the following chapters, we will be referring to our picture of past and present, echoing it at many points, and drawing concepts and criteria from it.

We can see that if proponents of the two styles were to teach the game, they would end up with quite different products. The proponents of the Big Game style would stress serve, volley, and attack *very early* in the teaching process. Here we must part company with them, for this approach is counter to the basic principles of this book—that tennis is taught on levels of play, that first things must always be first, that highly developed, competent groundstrokes are of prime importance. In the past or in the present, defense is the cornerstone of the game.

Tennis is properly taught on levels of play—beginner, intermediate, and advanced—and there are strategical frameworks (over-all plans for winning) that are appropriate to each level. Strokes and tactics, the patterns of play to carry out the winning plans, are taught within these frameworks. One of the many criteria for these strategical frameworks can be expressed simply—increasing degrees of ball control, which allow an increasing variety in the patterns of play.

Make no mistake: *the essence of the game is control.* This is what you are concerned with, day in and day out, on *all* levels of play, in teaching *all* equipment of the game. Your teaching of footwork, balance, rhythm, all basics and all dynamics and mechanics of the strokes, *everything*, is geared to this one purpose, controlling the ball.

This, to use a phrase of Wayne Sabin's, is "the shaping of the strokes," (forehands, backhands, volleys, and serves) the tools or equipment your pupils will use to play the game. It is the teaching of stroke production, but not in the sense of teaching fancy form or style, because strokes are meaningless unless the idea of ball control is built into them. Ball control, then, is the very heart of the game; without it any talk of strategy or tactics is pointless. The ball cannot even be placed somewhere in court without some mastery of control.

But just as it is useless to talk strategy and tactics without control, so it is futile to talk control without the winning plans and tactics in mind. We shape the strokes for one purpose: their use in the patterns of play (tactics), within the strategical framework that is appropriate for each level of play.

Ball control and tactics, then, are subtly intertwined. The kind of strategy and tactics we can teach on any level is partly dependent on ball control; further, the means we use to control the ball are dependent on the playing situation, and ball control and tactics have different meanings at each level of play. Together they form two closely connected routes

2 A FRAMEWORK FOR TEACHING

for the progressive development of a tennis player. Therefore, each section of this book is prefaced with a chapter called "The Strategical Framework." It is important for us to see clearly all the purposes for which we are developing the strokes. It is important for us to see ball control in terms of a progressive plan of development and to understand the relationship between ball control and tactics.

To define these progressive frameworks, we are concerned with two basic ideas—where a pupil can take a ball in his court, and where he can place it in his opponent's court. As a player progresses, he attains the kind of control that enables him to take the ball earlier and earlier; he develops the kind of control that enables him to use more and more of his opponent's court. As we saw in Chapter 1, these two skills are interrelated—the *earlier* a player can take the ball the *more he can use all of his opponent's court*. Thus the concepts of a gradually diminishing No-Man's-Land and a gradually increasing ability to probe more and more of an opponent's territory help to distinguish the three levels of play.

Now, what of the beginner? Our beginning player is never more than a groundstroker. He is thinking about all the basics and mechanics that help him gain control of the ball through the flat backhand and forehand drives and the flat beginning serve that we are teaching him. We will, of course, start him on learning the volley, but we must caution him that it is *not* a useful weapon in the beginning.

The fact that the beginner is learning to gain control over the ball dictates his playing position in the court. It is about six feet *behind the base line*. No-Man's-Land for him is vast, the area from six feet behind the base line to the net. Actually he will find the space back to the fence more useful than the forecourt and the net. On this basis his choice of shots and his patterns of play are rather limited. He has only one strategy—steadiness. Within this framework we will teach him tactics, but in the main the beginner is a pusher *par excellence*, or, as Chet Murphy calls him, a rallyer. And so the strategical framework for the beginner is steadiness, his own special kind of steadiness, however, always getting one more ball back into court.

From the standpoint of control, generally speaking, the intermediate is grooving his basic strokes. He is "feeling" the ball now because he is elongating his hitting area. He has learned to "carry the ball" on his racket, but, due to the new tactical situations that we place him in and the tactical situations that are forced on him by his opponents, he is now much more concerned with spin of the ball—topspin and underspin. Topspin is particularly important now because he is hitting the ball harder. "Pushing" has now changed to "sparring," particularly from backhand to backhand. *Ball speed*, of course, is one of the criteria for the levels of play, and the intermediate hits harder with less height but has not necessarily developed a knockout punch yet.

Fundamentally, there are three stages in the intermediate's development. The first we can call *transitional*. In this stage we will move him closer to the base line to test his control when he is hitting an earlier ball, and we will continue to work on smoothing out his strokes, eliminating any flaws that appeared in the beginning or that may have cropped up during competitive play. But it is important at this time to bring his volley up to the same standard as the groundstrokes and serve. As much as we may stress the groundstrokes, extreme neglect of the volley is a mistake. It takes the average pupil more time to become at home at the net than on the base line.

At the end of the transitional stage, our pupil is beginning to look like a tennis player. He is taking the ball far earlier, and, consequently, court position (in terms of the width of the court) becomes more and more important. We teach him now to match his position to his shot. In fact, we teach him to play *position* tennis, which tactically means cross-court hitting from the base line—deep cross-court shots into the corners. Our second-stage intermediate is far from an all-court player. Basically, he is now concentrating on *defensive* tennis, and therefore we will want to teach him underspin for use on the high backhand, the wide shot, and the return of serve.

It is in the third stage that the intermediate makes his first move toward *offensive* tennis. Now he will learn what Wayne Sabin calls the art of winning tennis—coming in behind the short ball. Volleying includes the determination of what ball to come in on, the technique and placement of the approach shot, and, finally, placement of the volley. All of this takes time to learn, and our intermediate will be working on it and, to a lesser extent, using it in his playing, in this stage. But despite his introduction to aggression, the intermediate is not an attacking player, and so the strategical framework at this point is *position tennis*.

In both beginning and intermediate tennis the progression is clear. Step by step we are leading the pupil to greater control and feeling in all the strokes. From steadiness he moves to deftness in defense, and at the end of the intermediate stage he should be equipped to become the all-court player.

Defining the advanced stage is not quite as simple. We have indicated that there are several directions in which a tennis player can go, depending on his individual make-up; therefore, it is best to leave the final definition of an advanced player to the following chapter, "Tennis Games Are Tailor-Made." There are some criteria, however, that apply to all advanced players. Generally speaking, an advanced player is in a period of consolidation. Chiefly through practice and tournament play, our advanced player is putting together all the pieces we have given him prior to this time, but three points in particular suggest progression at this stage, also. First, he is beginning to blend his backcourt, forecourt, and net play, and the very short ball he came in on as an intermediate is now a gradually lengthening short ball; second, he will be coming in behind his serve; in addition, the advanced player has become a "counterpuncher." These three factors add up to one thing—the advanced player is an *attacker as well as a defender*. He can play *pressure tennis;* quite possibly, he may be very much at home now in No-Man's-Land. Pressure tennis, then, is the strategical framework for this final stage of development.

So these are the strategical frameworks—steadiness, position, and pressure tennis—for each of the levels of play. These are the over-all plans for winning within which we teach tactics and ball control.

The coaching of any sport is most successful when individualized. Individual differences—mental, emotional, and physical—must always be considered. Tennis games are tailor-made to these differences in both strokes and strategy. All knowledge of stroke production and of strategy—the mechanics, the dynamics, defense and attack—becomes meaningful when applied to the individual. The teaching of tennis, then, is a creative job, and the relationship of individual differences to the many possibilities in strokes and strategy makes the teaching of the game fascinating as a student develops through the three levels of play.

When Welby Van Horn says, "None of my pupils end up hitting the ball exactly as I teach it," he is recognizing the importance of individual differences. He has made allowances for these differences in his teaching of ball control. Here we are talking about style. Style, in tennis as in everything else, is a particular flair in everything a person does, including the hitting of a tennis ball. Style is the personality of strokes, and the possibilities are legion.

All experienced teachers of tennis have their favorite look in the shape of the strokes; the differences, however, will be only in the variables, a type of backswing or ending, length and speed of swing, and so on. But all strokes will have one thing in common—soundness. The common denominator of soundness in all strokes is the action of the racket in the hitting area. It means proper contact of the racket on the ball to get a particular job done. It means ball control. Despite his preference in the shape of the strokes, the experienced teacher will allow the individual to stamp his own style on a basically sound stroke.

This individualization of hitting style may frequently begin quite early in the teaching process, but it will be most noticeable in the beginning of the intermediate stage. Each teacher must find his own way of handling individual style. Often

3 | TENNIS GAMES ARE TAILOR-MADE

there is a wide gap between our favorite picture of the strokes and the student's style. Sometimes we may feel that one of the arts of teaching strokes is the ability to curb all the natural instincts and tendencies, and we have good company. (There's a wonderful Ben Hogan story in which he was asked how to become a great golfer. "Very simple," he said. "Just go out and do everything that comes unnatural to you for ten years.")

In Part II–The Beginner we present a basic concept of control. In Part III—The Intermediate we will explore in depth the dynamics of hitting a tennis ball. It is from this enlarged range that you will choose the materials to adjust to individual differences. However, just as in the final analysis only playing the game makes a tennis player, so only teaching the game will bring the proficiency through experience that will enable you to make the right choices.

Tennis games are tailor-made not only in strokes but in patterns of play.

In all sports there are two basic stratagems—defense and offense—and all coaches agree that both are important. However, many coaches will favor one over the other, and, unfortunately, fads arise as current champions emphasize either an exceptional offense or an exceptional defense. Actually, there should be only one criterion for the degree to which a coach stresses each of the stratagems—the kind of player with which he is working. No two basketball or baseball teams should necessarily play the same way. If all-out attack is the ideal, it's unfortunate, because there just aren't enough all-court pressers and home-run kings to go around.

It is on the advanced level of play that the individualization of playing patterns occurs. Certainly through the first two levels of play we attempt to equip them to handle all phases of the game equally well, but sometimes they are unable to do this.

Ideally, we would like to find our advanced player a subtle defender who has developed touch, the ultimate in ball control; a steady baseliner, capable of using the whole court of his opponent; a patient, resourceful, thinking player who can find his opponents' second-best shots when no weaknesses appear; a player who realizes that there are other means with which to attack than a big serve and power and a volley; a player who knows how to play the big points, to change a losing game but always stick to a winning one; a player who knows the full value of attack at the right time; and one who knows that attack pays off on the faster surfaces (and so defense must be all the more important here, too).

Touch, in good part, is an inborn attribute. We can only foster it and develop it to the best of our ability through our teaching of ball control. And if not touch, what then? What if our player doesn't have enough of this inborn gift? Power, of course. We must recognize that all the equipment of the game can be great for two reasons—consistency and power. Very rarely are these two combined. Furthermore, patience and resourcefulness may be lacking as well as touch and consistency. A player's natural instinct may be to gamble.

There are often compensating strengths—individual strengths such as a big serve and power, an exceptional ability to volley. In this case, control on the groundstrokes is important only to the extent that a player can make enough telling blows to win the match. This kind of player will always have to count on the pressure of constant attack. His route in the final stage will be the Big Game.

All advanced players can do the same things; how well and how consistently they do them makes the difference between a good club, college, or park player and someone ranked among the top twenty players. For the good college player to try to play the Big Game when it is not his forte is a waste of talent. As Wayne Sabin says, "Too many players play the game the way they *think* it should be played, not as they should play it."

This book is not a plea for standardization in the teaching of the game (a plea we hear frequently); rather, it is a plea for flexibility in taking into account the many possibilities for play and the individual differences among players.

In teaching the strokes, every instructor must know how he wants them to look, and he must possess the ability to communicate it. Knowing the look we want stems from our knowledge of the basics, the dynamics, and the mechanics of stroke production. Communication involves the development of a personal teaching method, or approach, for developing the strokes and the use of checkpoints, cues, and corrective techniques.

Generally speaking, there are two methods for developing the strokes: (1) teaching the whole swing, and (2) teaching its parts (backswing, forward swing, point of contact, and follow-through).

In an ideal lesson, a teacher concentrates on the whole swing. The more natural ability a student has, the less often the instructor has to take up in detail the parts of the swing. The pleasant reminder, "swing the racket-head," is often all that is necessary to correct a fault in the stroke of the well-coordinated student who has an outline of the swing in mind; at other times, however—even with the talented pupil—it becomes necessary to explain and demonstrate carefully one part of the swing, or to concentrate on an unfirm wrist or on over-rotation. Nevertheless, it is important for the instructor to keep his novice aware of the whole swing at all times and to return to it as soon as possible.

Pauline Betz Addie, adhering to the first axiom in teaching the game, "keep it simple," expresses the general preference:

I prefer to teach the whole swing, but of course if a pupil has difficulty with *any* of the parts, and I cannot make the necessary corrections through the whole swing, I do not hesitate to use the parts approach.

Many teachers, however, go far beyond these two methods in developing techniques for teaching the game. These tech-

THE TEACHING PROCESS | 4

niques arise out of instructors' varying emphases on the basics (such as grips, balance, rhythm, concentration, footwork, and the hitting area). All instructors agree on the importance of basics, of course, but there are "purists" and "liberals" who value some basics more than they do others. Within their system they teach the dynamics (the forces that work on the ball: how to get topspin, underspin—in other words, how to get ball control), and the mechanics (the mechanical details of the stroke—the length of the backswing, the position of an elbow, body rotation, and so on.)

For example, we use the phrase "swing the racket-head" as a cue to get that easy racket-does-the-work look that is the hallmark of most good players. Now, one concept of the stroke is that it is a swing, that "swinging the racket-head" is one of the most important things in stroke production. We have now elevated our cue to a basic. We can explain how balance, rhythm, timing, are included in the concept of swing. We explain how "not swinging" may cause mechanical difficulties. The principle of centrifugal force is the heart of this teaching method, and there are many teachers who use it, although it is used more frequently in golf than in tennis.

A brief view of some of these teaching techniques (all developed at length later in this book) will clarify the picture of varying emphasis on the basics.

One example is Welby Van Horn's important and impressive development of a whole system of teaching the strokes through one basic—*balance*. Certainly no word in a teacher's vocabulary is more important than balance. Watch a good quarterback in action, a basketball player as he moves to make a jump shot, or two boxers in the ring—they all have balance. We recognize its importance, but few of us have used the concept as precisely as Van Horn does.

When you read about Van Horn's Balance Approach, you will notice that there is no mention of the shaping of the stroke; he is talking about balance, pure and simple. Since balance can be taught and practiced even without a racket we might think at first that it does not have anything to do with "shaping the strokes," but when Van Horn forms the essentials of good balance, *he is automatically shaping the stroke.* He creates a frame, or "mold," in which to put the racket. Once the pupil has absorbed the principles of the Van Horn Balance Approach, a few key ideas on the swing will set him well on his way.

Another extremely sound approach is Dennis Van der Meer's Rhythm Approach. Rhythm, like balance, is one of the essentials of the game. In addition to being a good example of a personal teaching technique, this approach is noteworthy for two other reasons. It eliminates the frustration many pupils experience when taught in the very beginning to hit from baseline to baseline, and it dovetails with one of the basic premises of this book, that ball control is tailor-made to the playing situation: Van der Meer highlights our point that the size of the stroke is dependent on the job at hand.

In utilizing the rhythm approach, Van der Meer paves the way for the teaching of the volley and the approach shot.

Still another example is the Hitting Area Technique, which emphasizes racket control in the approach to the ball, contact, and follow-through. The Hitting Area Approach is important because it highlights point of impact, of which Wayne Sabin says,

...the thing that is most noticeable about the experienced player is *how he does dignify the point of impact, how he does respect it and devote all his concentration to that instant.*

Chet Murphy says,

After all, what's done before contact is preparatory. The backswing and forward swing are merely to get the racket to the beginning of the "gun barrel," and many kinds of backswing are permissible to do this job. The ending of the stroke is merely an automatic outgrowth of the action in this control area. I use this approach to explain how little importance need be attached to the kinds of backswing and all the fancy endings.

And finally, as Bill Murphy says, "What happens in the hitting area is really the essence of the stroke. Too few players are aware of the Hitting Area concept, possibly because it has not been stressed enough."

It is through these over-all approaches that we communicate some of our basic concepts of the strokes, but within these approaches we rely on checkpoints, cues, and corrective techniques to help us achieve the correct shape of the strokes.

Chet Murphy defines checkpoints as "the features on which a teacher can ascertain the degree to which an individual's stroke conforms to the desired pattern. The start of the backswing and the point at which it ends, the start of the forward swing, the point of contact, the follow-through, and the finish position are generally regarded as ordinary checkpoints in a single stroke."

He says this of cues:

How can the learner best be guided in this practice in which he attempts to modify every unsuccessful execution? The learner responds to verbal cues made by the teacher. The cues, of course, must be carefully selected and must be in keeping with the general method of stroking recommended by the teacher. "Elbow down at the finish," for example, could be a valuable guide to a beginner who tends to turn the racket over in contradiction to the teacher's instructions to "finish with the racket face perpendicular to the ground."

But "keeping the elbow down" may not mean the same thing to every pupil, nor may it be equally effective in developing proper form with every pupil. To some pupils there may be a better way of saying what there is to say about the kind of finish required. Perhaps "stand the racket on edge" will serve the purpose, or "don't roll the wrist" may do it.

The teacher must say the same thing in as many different ways as he can in order to reach as many of his pupils as possible. He must also define his terms so that they mean exactly what he wants them to mean to his pupils. In the final analysis, what a learner does depends on how he interprets the instructions.

Often it is not what we say, but what we get as a result that counts. Welby Van Horn, offers a most important contribution regarding both checkpoints and cues. He advises his pupils to be their own critics. He says,

Many instructors emphasize certain checkpoints in their teaching. I do, most emphatically. I also constantly repeat key phrases (cues) in emphasizing what I consider to be important parts of proper balance, grips, strokes, and tactics. If these checkpoints and key phrases are firmly etched in a pupil's mind, he will be able to practice correctly without the constant attention of an instructor. Remember, practice does not necessarily make perfect; only *correct* practice produces improvement, and the checkpoints and key phrases will enable your pupils to eventually assemble the pieces of the jig-saw puzzle which represent all the elements of balance, grips, strokes, and tactics.

Finally, nothing is more important than the ability to use corrective techniques. Van der Meer says of this area of work,

Imagination and experience are the two prerequisites for making successful corrections. My philosophy in corrective technique is that the more dramatic and meaningful a suggestion can be made, the quicker a pupil will respond and the longer he will remember it. Each of us must develop his own ability to recognize faults and then either use existing techniques or invent our own. But corrective techniques should not be attempted until the teacher has a preconceived picture of every shot, and the teacher must be flexible enough to allow for individual differences from his preconceived picture in every case that arises.

If corrective work is the order of the lesson, Van der Meer ends the lesson by reviewing the corrective suggestions; the pupil knows precisely the improvement Van der Meer wants to see by the next lesson.

Checkpoints, cues, and corrective techniques—these are the tools we use to communicate. The ideal way for pupils to learn is through imitation, provided they have the right things to imitate, but only a talented few can learn this way. Most of the time we must tell pupils what we want and what we don't want, which illustrates our point that the teaching of tennis is a creative job. It requires imagination to select and use the right cues and to invent proper corrective techniques for each individual we teach.

However, let's not lose sight of that axiom we discussed at the beginning of this chapter—keep it simple. One step at a time is enough. The one right step at the one right time, the idea of progression, is an important basic premise. Teaching the right stroke or tactic at the right time produces a sound foundation to which the blocks are added, one by one. Van Horn expresses the idea this way: "We never put the pupil in a situation that he can't handle." But at the right time, we are always ready to present the new challenges that make the game exciting. This gradual unfolding of all the possibilities in the game is food for growth, stimulus for development.

And so, there is a time and place for everything—a time for speed, a time for spin, a place for open footwork, a place for attack as well as for defense.

Finally, there is one key to the use of all the teaching materials of the game —adapt your teaching to individual skill and progress.

The Beginner

A. Ball Control

Teaching beginners does not require a vast knowledge of spin of the ball, but it does require a knowledge of control. This statement may appear to be contradictory because "spinning the ball" and "controlling the ball" have become somewhat synonymous. However, this kind of thinking can lead to a fallacy in the early shaping of the groundstrokes: the idea that the racket has to be consciously turned over the ball or brushed up the back of the ball to get topspin for control. Actually, this emphasis can cause unsteadiness in the beginning player, by lessening contact between the racket strings and the ball.

The racket does not have to be turned over or brushed up the ball for control, although some good teachers do use one or the other method with success. For instance, one of the outstanding teachers of the game teaches flicking the racket over the ball with the fingers, but he is a master at this tricky type of teaching, and we had best leave it to him. Nor will we argue the point that "covering the ball" has a place in the teaching of the groundstrokes. It is a highly legitimate technique when used in the right way, and we will discuss it in Part III.

Even if you do not over-teach topspin in the early shaping of the strokes, you may have anxious pupils on the other side of the net who possess a natural tendency to use one or the other of the above methods to get a ball over the net and place it some sixty to eighty feet away. They may compound this by hitting too hard, failing to recognize that the law of gravity will work for them if they can refrain from powdering the ball, and that they have an ally here that eliminates the necessity of complicated racket attempts to spin the ball.

This is not to say that some topspin is not desirable on the basic backhand and forehand drives. What is important is

THE STRATEGICAL
FRAMEWORK
5

how it is obtained and how much of it is applied at the beginning level. We are aspiring now to teach control in the simplest possible way. This is why most of us teach a flat shot in the beginning—not flat in terms of height over the net, nor with an absolutely spinless ball (because there is no such thing), nor in the style of backswing. The flatness is in the racket face as it contacts the ball (on the waist-high ball, the racket face is perpendicular to the court surface), and in the shape of the stroke in the hitting area. Yet, in the latter case, "flat" can be a word we use to offset the picture of too much topspin because actually there is an upward action of the racket in the hitting area.

Before we begin to develop the strokes for our beginner, let's discuss our basic concept of ball control. Remember: the strategical framework is *steadiness*; therefore, control of the groundstrokes and the serve, the three strokes we are concerned with at the start, must be built around the idea of steadiness. The very heart of control on all three levels of play is watching the ball. From the very beginning, concentration on the ball is a requisite. Centered hitting is a must. With this always in mind, we concentrate first on keeping an approximately flat racket face at point of contact and throughout the follow-through on both the forehand and backhand, and a flat racket face at point of contact on the serve.

The rest of our teaching of the groundstrokes can be conveyed in one sentence: swing slightly up and *carry* the ball into the court. Because we want that ball from five to fifteen feet up or higher for beginners, we teach a slightly upward swing, a swing that starts just barely below the ball at the end of the backswing and continues in a straight upward path through the ball. Once the ball is up, what brings it down? Very simple. The same upward swing. If you are fortunate enough to have one teaching ball that has a trace of its trademark left, use it to show a pupil this principle. Hold it in your left hand between the thumb and forefinger with the trademark up, and show them how it rotates when you swing the flat racket face slightly upward into the ball. This is topspin, just enough to do the job in the beginning when it is coupled with easy hitting and the force of gravity.

What we have here is a simple basic picture of control—a flat racket swinging slightly upward into the ball, setting an upward trajectory and automatically adding enough topspin for the beginner. The word "carry" conveys an image that is the main key to control. We want the pupil to *carry* the ball into court, to keep it on his racket for a long time. An elongated hitting area is essential to success on the groundstrokes, and the reason for teaching this flat stroke is that it does provide the largest hitting area.

There is a hitting area on the serve, too, although we may not use the idea with serves as frequently as we do with the groundstrokes. "Up and out" is always the cue on the serve, and "flat" is the word for the beginner. Only on the volley is there a variation on this theme. This stroke is downward; the racket face is open.

Often we may get what we want by telling our pupil what we don't want. We *don't* want them to brush the ball on the groundstrokes, to take a glancing strike at the ball, one that starts too low and ends too high. We *don't* want them consciously turning the racket over the ball. A turning racket demands too precise a point of contact. Brushing the ball means too little contact of strings and ball and tends to eliminate the follow-through. With the racket face approximately flat at point of contact and throughout the follow-through, the ball can be controlled, and the chances of staying with the ball are greater if the swing is only slightly upward. This same principle applies to the serve. All the complications involved in slicing, overspinning, or twisting the ball affect consistency. A direct strike at the ball is the quickest route to ball control on the groundstrokes and the serve.

B. Ball Control and Beginning Tactics

Some may consider it heresy to talk so much about control in a day when speed is king on the tennis court, but tennis is won mainly on an opponent's errors; aces and placements play only a small part in the final tally. Control of the ball, then, must be an important factor—yet all we see and hear today is speed and more speed. We are told that speed is the ideal towards which we have been building over the years. McLaughlin started the trend back in 1912; Tilden, Vines, and Budge furthered it, and Kramer climaxed the process with the Big Game. And so now, as a result of Kramer's brilliance, the power pattern has become so dominant that it has begun to affect all areas of the game—off the ground, at the net, on the serve, and even in the warm-up.

Another tendency is taking the ball earlier and earlier. Cochet, in 1924, said that the future of the game was in taking the ball on the rise. Very good. But Cochet was talking about *advanced*, not *beginning*, tennis, and he did not necessarily mean that the ball should be taken on the rise only to gain more speed. The chief advantages, he believed, lay in the player's opportunities to control the play and take advantage of angles, but taking the ball early is not an "Open Sesame" to controlling the play, because we cannot control the play if we cannot control the ball.

Ball control is so closely related to tactics that the two become inseparable on all levels of play. Its importance to the development of a beginner's game can best be explained through a discussion of beginning strategy and tactics.

The strategy is steadiness;
the first tactic is depth;
the second tactic is playing a backhand.

We can, if we want, call these the three stages of beginning tennis. For any player in the beginning, there can be only steadiness. A nine-year-old playing the Big Game would be about as effective as a midget rushing the net against Emerson. This is a time for just getting balls back, *high* up over the net—ten feet, fifteen or twenty feet, perhaps. Who cares how high, as long as they go in? Beginners are all unsullied innocents who have never heard of the Big Game, and they couldn't play it if they had. As a matter of fact, beginners' tennis is kind of fun to watch: tennis balls just going somewhere into court. No zip, zip, serve, and return error; no bang, bang, passing shot, and volley error. Just up and over and in—a couple of kids trying to control the ball, just hitting it somewhere into court.

There are five important points for your pupil to learn while he is acquiring steadiness and the two beginning tactics: (1) early preparation, (2) point of contact in relation to the bounce, (3) point of contact in relation to his body, (4) a slow, easy swing, and (5) the part played by the force of gravity.

In the beginning, nothing is more important than hitting the ball after it has come down from the top of the bounce, hitting it waist-high or lower. Often this means a willingness to scoot back to the fence in order to give the high-bouncing baseline shots enough time to come down. Of course, some attention must be given to getting back to home base, a spot in the middle of the court about six feet behind the baseline, but for some time to come, position in relation to the bounce of the ball is much more important to the beginner than court position. Maintaining this kind of position to the bounce of the ball will facilitate preparation. All beginners are poor preparers (a fault often seen in intermediate and advanced players, too), and because of this, the more time they have to prepare, the better. Hitting on the rise, or the top of the bounce, does not give them proper time for preparation; consequently, they are forced because of late preparation to swing the racket too fast, a surefire route to inconsistency.

Even with early preparation, one of the most difficult tasks your beginner will have is learning to swing the racket slowly enough to control the ball. "Killing" the ball is fun on any level of play, of course. Home runs are more fun than base hits, too, but home runs are as rare as placements in tennis, and the steady output of balls into court pays off in the end. Depending on how grooved the stroke is, there is a certain speed at which a player can swing the racket and control it, and hence control the ball. It is important for your pupil to know his speed from the beginning. When he understands that it is *efficiency* of swing, not muscle, that gets power, he has made real progress. Chet Murphy sums it up this way: "If they feel that they are straining to hit hard, then they are trying to hit *too* hard. Speed should come from a smooth, easy, well-coordinated swing, not from straining, grunting, or groaning. *We want a controlled shot, so we teach a controlled swing.*"

The easy swinging of the racket is tied in with the last of our five points—

the part played by the force of gravity. In beginning tennis, it is actually more important than topspin. If the ball is hit over the net easily enough, it will go into court regardless of what kind of spin has been put on the ball. And this is what the first stage of beginning tennis is all about—a couple of kids taking the correct grip on their rackets, getting the rackets back early, letting the ball come down, and swinging up through the ball so easily that the force of gravity causes it to land somewhere in court. And this is precisely what the beginner is doing on the serve in this initial stage of development; he is merely attempting to get the ball somewhere into the service area.

As your beginner progresses, however, "somewhere in court" is not good enough, and one of the great tactics on any level of play, depth, becomes a must. Depth, of course, is important through all stages of development because it keeps an opponent on the defensive. Transition to depth is easy if there has been due emphasis on steadiness in early training and sound shaping of the strokes. Easy and high are basic to depth at this stage, and flat strokes with a long hitting area lend themselves to depth very readily. The background is right for controlling the ball into the baseline. It may go into the backhand or forehand or into the middle of the court, but it will go deep, into an area three to eight feet from the baseline.

More and more our beginner is learning to use the racket head to hit the ball. Actually, the hand is developing an affinity for the baseline, the same kind of affinity that a basketball player gets for the basket. But, just as you can't shoot them in on a straight line, you can't hit them deep on a straight line either, so let's continue to keep height over the net in mind. In this second stage, the pupil may attempt to serve the first ball into the backhand, but the second ball should not be placed. It should be merely *in*.

The second tactic—playing an opponent's backhand—involves placement, a somewhat more difficult task for the beginner, both mechanically and psychologically. Most beginners must be weaned away from playing the ball safely down the middle. To convince them of the importance of concentrated effort on playing an opponent's backhand, you might express it as Chet Murphy does: "Make believe your opponent has a big yellow and black sign on his left shoulder that reads: WEAK BACKHAND! PLEASE DON'T HIT THE BALL HERE! And so, of course, you hit most of them there, particularly to get out of trouble."

Deep, wide trouble on the forehand side may best be answered by hitting into the center or cross-court, however. And the deeper and wider the shots, the higher the ball should go. There is no point in threading a needle down the sideline when the safest shot is cross-court. Our beginner will always attempt to hit his backhand deep cross-court, however, and in doing so will be practicing what many call the one most important groundstroke shot in the game.

Deep straight shots and occasional deep cross-courts from the forehand, deep cross-courts from the backhand—this is the choice of shots for the beginner, with particular emphasis on the cross-court backhand and the straight forehands to play that inviting weakness. This is his only concern with placement. To perform these shots, as Chet Murphy observes, the beginner "must know *his* point of contact for straight-ahead shots and so be able to vary contact for other placements." Although the direction of the swing and the slant of the racket influences direction, point of contact is the main key to placement. And it is a somewhat personal thing, involving as it does the type of grips used and the amount of rotation and weight-shift. For the two placements—cross-court and down the line—we express points of contact loosely, as early and late, respectively. And these placements are off a straight-ahead point of contact that might be approximately from opposite the left hip to two inches in front of the toes of the left foot, on the forehand, and from opposite the right hip to about a foot in front of the toes of the right foot, on the backhand. And finally, in this last stage, the pupil should place both first and second serves into the backhand.

Placement of return of serve follows our pattern precisely. First, the pupil returns serve anywhere into court. As he progresses he attains depth and, finally, the ability to hit into his opponent's backhand. The high backhand is the most difficult shot for his opponent to return, so we suggest to our pupils, as Chet Murphy does, "make your opponent go back for a backhand."

Now that we have stated a basic concept of control and indicated the purposes for which we will be shaping all the beginner's strokes, we are ready to develop a beginning player.

But one final note of caution before we proceed. Despite our concern with control and steadiness, all of us like power. But we do not like uncontrolled power that comes from consciously stepped up hitting, which can cause an abrupt change in the shape of the stroke. Power should come from a smooth transfer of energy and the smooth application of pressure to the ball at point of contact. Power comes from efficiency of swing. And so, at the beginning, as Van Horn puts it, "Power is a word that should be eliminated from our pupil's tennis vocabulary. It will appear magically in due time if he adheres to the fundamentals of balance and proper stroking." In addition to power, we all like early hitting, as early as a player's reactions and ball control will allow. It is, of course, an aid to speed. More important, it is a sure path to controlling the play. It is also essential to the sound position play that we will require of our intermediate player. Both speed and early hitting, however, should be continuously curtailed in the early stages of development. If your player has been taught the basic pattern of controlling the ball, then the transition to speed and early hitting will occur automatically as he advances.

If there is one thing we have in this game, it's grips! We have the Western, the modified Western, the Eastern, the Composite, the Semi-Continental, the Continental, and many more. All these grips are actually used (to some degree), and, concerning any one of them, I doubt that any two professionals would agree as to the exact position for the fingers, the V between the first finger and the thumb and the heel of the hand. We all agree on one grip that is wrong: the fingers are close together, the heel of the hand is on top of the handle. It's called the Hatchet grip. None of us would teach this, so nobody uses it. Well, with just one exception—a well-known pusher of recent years from California, fellow by the name of Gonzales.

So, what's in a grip?

Not long ago, the top Americans were critical of the Australians because they used the Continental grip. When the fifth Australian won the American Championships, one of those critics (an all-time great) said, in reporting the match, "You know, I've come around to thinking that the Continental grip may not be too much of a disadvantage."

But we got out of that one nicely. We decided to call it the Composite grip. It was not quite Continental—it was a cross between the Continental and the Eastern.

So, what's in a grip?

Well, quite a bit, actually.

For instance, grips affect the shape of the stroke. In fact, when we talk about grips as widely divergent as the Western and Continental, we are talking about two very different styles of swinging. Moreover, each grip has a different feel at contact. Each grip affects the spin of the ball in a different manner. The style of play and the court surfaces also affect the choice of grips. One grip will be better for high bounces, another for low. The increased tempo of the modern style of play has dictated less and less grip change from forehand to

GRIPS 6

backhand, both on the groundstrokes and at the net. And finally, one grip may allow more finger control over the racket than another. Looking at the extremes, the Western is very much a palm grip; the Continental is the extreme example of a finger grip.

Obviously, grips are important!

To say that you can't hit a stroke with this or that grip is not so. To say that you can't apply underspin with this or that grip is not so, either. We have only to look at the wide range of grips used on the forehands, from Billy Johnston (Western) to Fred Perry (Continental) to Gonzales (Hatchet), to know that diversity of grips is possible. The same applies to the backhands of Tilden (full Eastern), Budge (less Eastern), and Rosewall (Composite). Nevertheless, we can talk about a "range of correctness," as Chet Murphy does.

Just what is the purpose of a grip? Well, one simple explanation of the groundstrokes is that we hit a ball with the palm of our hand on the forehand, the back of our hand on the backhand; it follows that the racket is an extension of the forearm in either case. You might move so far toward the Continental grip that the racket head ends well in front of the arm; or you might move well toward the Western grip, so that the racket head is well behind the arm. Certainly both of these grips would be outside our range of correctness. The grip, then, should make the racket as much an extension of the arm as possible.

But there is a more subtle reason for the choice of grips.

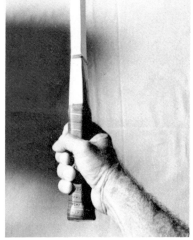

Eastern Forehand, Also the Intermediate Service Grip.

Western Forehand, Also the Beginner's Service Grip.

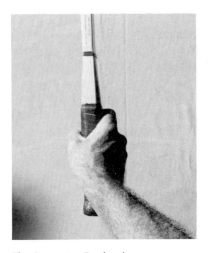

The Composite Forehand.

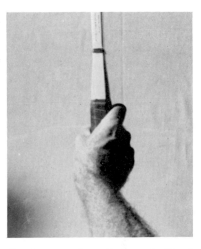

The Continental or Eastern Backhand Grip, Also the Advanced Service Grip.

Van Horn says,

I firmly believe there is such a thing as a "tennis hand," just as there is a perfect "piano hand," "guitar hand" or "violin hand." I have purposely used the simile of stringed instruments because a tennis racket is in this category, too, and this leads to one of the key words in my teaching—touch.

A touch "feeling" comes from the fingers. Touch means a "feel" detection. Through the grip, the feeling of impact on the ball demands a sensitive touch, also. Touch determines the ability to control the ball—especially the control that requires good depth of the stroked ball. It is, of course, necessary to the mastery of the more delicate shots in tennis, i.e., drop shots, lobs, drop volleys, and lob volleys. Touch, to a great extent, designates the calibre of a player. It is an inherent quality, but it can be acquired to a degree through proper grips. Certainly it is more readily transferred to the ball with the proper grips.

Unfortunately, the proper groundstroke grips (Eastern for both forehand and backhand) will not always feel natural to the beginner. The average beginner will want to use the Western grip for the forehand and something close to the Eastern forehand grip for the backhand. So one of our early tasks is the constant checking of grips. The purist will be more insistent that the precisely orthodox grip be used; the liberal will compromise up to the point at which the grip begins to affect the shape of the stroke adversely.

When the full Eastern grip for the backhand is taught, there is always some concern about the placement of the thumb. There are three possibilities— straight up the handle, diagonal, or wrapped around the handle. Thumb position is optional, but minor distinctions can be made. Straight up may produce better racket control for the beginner, whereas the third grip will allow more wrist freedom at a later stage.

Most certainly, the proper service grip must develop gradually. Few teachers would consider starting the beginner with an advanced service grip. Rather, they will teach almost a full Western grip for the serve in the beginning, gradually moving the pupil toward the grip he will use as an advanced player.

The volleying grips for the beginner are the same as the forehand and backhand grips. Most beginners and intermediates will get better results on the volley with a change of grips from backhand to forehand. In the advanced stage, they may find more success using a single grip.

Despite the fact that all the grips mentioned at the beginning of this chapter are usable, we recommend that for the forehand you teach either the Eastern or the Composite grip (the heel of the hand placed on the top plane of the racket), and for the backhand we recommend the Eastern grip, which can also be called the full Continental.

A. The Forehand Drive

(*Bill Murphy*)

In deciding on a starting point in the teaching of tennis strokes, I have, like most teachers of the game, chosen the forehand ground stroke. I have done so because I feel that it is the most important stroke to learn from a beginner's point of view. He will learn the forehand quicker and achieve more using it than any other area of the game.

I start my beginners by having them try to rally, either on the court or against a wall, in any manner they desire—any grip, any stance, any swing. I do this to let them get the feel of the equipment, some knowledge of the flight and bounce of the ball, and some respect for the difficulty involved in hitting a controlled ball. I assume they have a rudimentary idea of the purpose of the game. If they do not, I spend a little time explaining the game, using chalk-drawn diagrams to illustrate.

Next, I demonstrate and explain the swing we will be learning. I hit self-dropped balls first, then tossed balls (I have the pupil stand at the net and toss to me), while standing a foot or two behind the center of the base line. I then demonstrate how one usually has to run to a ball, or at least move a little, because a ball seldom comes directly at a player. All hits and swings are done at reasonably slow speed so that the movements can be clearly discerned. While demonstrating, I explain my concept of the stroke, avoiding detailed explanations at this point. "Shake-hands grip with last three fingernails facing the net," "sideways stance," "semicircular backswing with a downward loop at its end," "flat, slightly rising forward swing," "swing through the ball," "racket on edge," and "reach and point toward the left net post" are the checkpoints I stress.

I then move on to practice-swing drills in which the student

SHAPING THE GROUNDSTROKES 7

Beginning of Inside-Out Swing.

Through the Hitting Area.

End of Stroke.

stands against a wall (or the net or a fence), about twelve inches from it, with his back to it. I explain to him that he is in a position to hit a ball to his left, parallel to the wall. After showing him, I then explain the grip to him, and I have him assume the proper grip on the racket. I then teach him my version of the forehand swing, making frequent use of my check-points. He learns the swing in this back-to-the-wall position, using the wall as a guide. He swings at an imaginary waist-high ball, letting the racket

The Low Forehand.

head, or the extreme tip of it, just barely touch the wall at the racket-back position and again at the finish-of-swing position.

My reason for using the wall is that it teaches a beginner that he must maintain control over the racket with a firm grip and firm wrist. He must "fight" the momentum of the swinging racket, as it is swung backward and then forward, to keep the racket from banging against the wall.

The wall serves as a guide, too, in teaching the amount of body pivot I recommend. As the racket is brought backward and upward with a slightly bent right arm, I want the right shoulder to move *toward* the wall and the left shoulder to move *away* from the wall, so that as the racket tip touches the wall the right shoulder is slightly closer to the wall than is the left shoulder.

At the completion of the swing, as the racket tip touches the wall in the opposite direction, the position of the shoulders is reversed: the left shoulder is now closer to the wall—much closer—than is the right shoulder.

I frequently draw X's on the wall, one where I want the racket to touch the wall in the racket-back position (with the player's arm slightly bent at the elbow), and the other where I want the racket to touch the wall at finish-position (with the player's arm fairly straight, in a modified reaching position).

At this point, too, I stress the all-important concept of stepping with the front foot *before* swinging the racket. "The step just barely precedes the swing," and "step, then swing" are the cues I use here.

I follow this drill with self-dropped hits against the fence or wall. The pupil flips the ball up to about shoulder height while standing in the sideways hitting position so that it strikes the ground about two feet in front of his left foot, toward an imaginary left net post. As the ball rises to its peak and begins to fall, he takes his racket back as he pivots at the hips. He steps forward as the ball bounces and then swings his racket forward to hit directly opposite his left hip, timing the swing so that he hits the ball just as it stops in midair. If the upward toss has been made properly—about shoulder high and about two feet in front of the left toe—he will make contact with the ball about waist-high and about opposite his left hip. I encourage him to pivot from the hips up during the forward swing so that at the completion of the stroke his shoulders are facing toward the wall or fence. Corrections in his swing are made as necessary during this drill, slowly and carefully, *one thing at a time*. He may have to regress to practice swings without the ball for a while to iron out the difficulties that have arisen.

Frequently, especially if the student is having difficulty learning the "step, then swing" concept, I'll have him hit the ball with the palm of his hand rather than with his racket. Frequent remainders to step and *then* swing often correct the faulty movement of swinging while stepping. I want the front foot *not* in midair but on the ground before the racket is swung forward.

My next step is to have the student hit the self-dropped ball to a target, in an attempt to make him conscious of control and accuracy and to convince him that the ball must be *stroked*, not slapped, to acquire control over it. I'll have him hit to a target (a circle or square) mounted or drawn on the wall first, and then to me as I stand against the wall acting as the target. While he hits, I stress the checkpoints, emphasizing particularly sound ball contact, using the cues "steer the ball" or "guide the ball toward the target."

I next introduce the pupil to the waiting position, in which he faces the net, and I teach him to turn from this position into the sideways hitting position. Practice-swing drills in this position are followed by drills in which the student flips the ball up into the air again and hits it against the wall. He'll quickly learn that moving to the ball, or footwork, is an important part of tennis. Because not all of his tosses will be in exactly the same place, he'll be getting some practice in adjusting his step to the position of the ball, and in many cases he will actually be moving from his starting position to a new, though not too distant, position. At this point additional explanation, description, and demonstration of the proper footwork are almost always necessary. Moving to the ball is new and strange to most beginners, whose previous experience in ball games, limited as it may be, was confined to baseball, in which *the ball comes to the hitter*. The concept of *the hitter going to the ball* is usually a strange one and must be worked on carefully, sometimes for a considerable time, before good footwork is combined with good balance and proper stroke execution.

The next step, obviously, is hitting tossed balls. This requires additional footwork practice: moving to the side, moving forward, moving backward, and moving obliquely forward and backward, just as one must do in actual play. I usually toss balls over the net to the student while standing three or four feet from the net. He stands on the opposite base line in the waiting position. The tosses are made slowly, so that he has time to run to the ball, to stop, and to hit it. I stress "run-stop-hit" with beginners to emphasize that they must maintain good hitting position and good balance during the swing. I'm not too fussy about accuracy during the early stages of this drill because the student is having a difficult time learning to *judge* and *time* the tossed ball and is usually lost in concentration on this one aspect. Later, however, when he has learned not to overrun the ball and not to force himself to reach for it, and when he is able to position himself properly so that he can make racket contact with the ball in his "strike zone" (between shoulder-height and knee-height), I begin, again, to stress accuracy and control by suggesting that he hit to the target, to me. I stress the "strike zone" concept here, urging him to get into position to play a *dropping* ball in his strike zone.

At this point I often ask him to place his racket aside and run to the ball, merely catching it so that he can catch the ball in his strike zone. I'll have him hit the ball, then, with the palm of his hand, asking him to "pose for a picture" at the end of the swing. I then have him resume hitting with the racket.

Next, I move back to just inside the base line and drop and hit a ball to him. Some balls will be hit directly to him (if I'm lucky!), so that he need take only a step or two to play them. Others I hit away from him, so that he has to run to play them. I try to vary the depth of my hits somewhat but not so much that I force him into an awkward, uncomfortable court position; here I introduce him to the idea of returning to "home base," the center of the baseline, after every hit. I encourage him to skip back to home base, using the sideward skip steps, suggesting that while skipping he keep his eyes on the ball that he has just hit.

We finally move on to the final step, rallying. We stand on opposite sides of the net, about two feet behind our respective center marks. I start the rally by dropping a ball and hitting it to him. He tries to return it to me, playing it on the first bounce. I return his hit, and the rally continues. I stress steadiness first, at this stage, then control (depth and accuracy), and finally, speed. Continued emphasis on good balance ("run-stop-hit"), a good finish ("reaching and pointing toward the left net post"), and a return to mid-court ("back to home base") is usually necessary at this point.

As we rally I present my concept of handling low and high balls, knee-high or lower to shoulder-high. I feel that the knees should be bent *regardless of the level of the ball*. They should be bent a great deal for low balls and only slightly for high ones. It is my belief that the racket head must be dropped for very low balls. It is virtually impossible to keep the racket handle parallel to the ground when playing a ball that is four or five inches above ground level. Pictures of leading players show that while they bend their knees for low balls, they also drop the racket head slightly. This is done not by loosening the grip or letting the wrist drop, but by pointing the arm slightly downward toward the ground. The racket head will be below the wrist, as it must be for very low balls. Also, the right shoulder will be lower than the left.

High balls are handled by moving the arm upward while maintaining the proper angle between the racket handle and forearm. The racket head will be well above the wrist. The trajectory of the swing would be slightly downward, naturally, with the left shoulder lower than the right.

Before I introduce a pupil to actual competitive play I give him considerable practice in returning serves. I'll serve easily at first, gradually picking up the speed of the serve, varying the spin and placement somewhat, to introduce him to the problem of judging the bounce of a served ball. He'll be asked only to return the serve at first, and then to return the serve and move immediately to home base.

This, in general, is the progression I follow in teaching the forehand. It is not my intention to suggest that the plan works as easily as I might have made it appear. There is no simple formula for developing any tennis stroke. The pitfalls are numerous, and considerable time must be spent correcting flaws that suddenly emerge in a seemingly well-learned stroke, reviewing simple basic movements, and reinforcing correct responses to the teaching cues used. Encouragement and cajolement, praise and criticism, humor and enthusiasm—these are the devices successful teachers use to make the learning process a fruitful one. The degree to which they must be used varies with each pupil, and the successful teacher is constantly striving to find which device, or which combination of devices, works best with each pupil.

The steps I follow are not foolproof, by any means. Yet, one needs a plan, a blueprint, to build the foundation of a sound stroke, and this is my method.

FOREHAND CHECKPOINTS

The Grip:

1. Midpoint of V or U formed by thumb and forefinger is on midpoint of top of handle if racket face is perpendicular to the ground, "standing on its edge."
2. First finger is spread in "trigger-finger" position.
3. Thumb is between first finger and middle finger, resting against side or middle finger.
4. Fingernails of last three fingers are facing the net.
5. Heel of hand rests on top of handle just forward of handle butt.

The Stance:

1. Stand sideways, like a batter in baseball.
2. Face the right sideline.
3. Keep weight on right foot.

The Backswing:

1. Hold racket face perpendicular to the ground, standing on its edge.
2. Use semicircular swing, with racket head moving backward about head high, elbow about chest high.
3. Take racket back to where the number 7 on a clock face would be (if 12 and 6 form a perpendicular to the net).
4. Keep wrist firm.

The Forward Swing:

1. Step forward before you swing.
2. Swing to hit a "low line drive," by dropping the arm and racket smoothly to just barely below the level at which the ball is to be hit.
3. Keep the racket standing on its edge.
4. Flatten out the arc of the swing. Move the right elbow past and away from the body.
5. Contact the ball about opposite the left hip.
6. Hit the ball "for a long time." Don't slap at it; hit it for as long as you can with a firm wrist.
7. Guide the ball; steer it.

The Finish of the Swing:

1. Point and reach toward the left net post, with the shoulders facing the net.
2. "Pose for a picture" for three seconds. (Count "one thousand one, one thousand two, one thousand three.")
3. Maintain a high, tight, firm finish with good balance.

B. The Backhand Drive

(Pauline Betz Addie)

"It's the easiest shot in the game," is my feeling about the backhand. And so it is—if you already have invested about ten years in the game of tennis.

I think back to my early tournament days when I had absolutely no backhand but was fast enough to cover both sides of the court with my forehand. When I was fourteen I was fortunate enough to watch Don Budge play in a Pacific Southwest Tournament in Los Angeles and was fascinated by the power and depth of his backhand. For the entire week of the tournament I went to bed dreaming of that great stroke, and for the next few years I tried my best to emulate the way his entire body seemed to flow into the swing. I finally reached a state where I would gladly run around my forehand to hit the backhand and have felt that way ever since.

Beginners shy away from the backhand because it seems to be an unnatural swing. Also, it is extremely difficult for a right-handed player to judge the ball on his left side. Anything that he does, such as throwing a baseball or even sweeping the floor, is done on the right side.

I go in slow steps when teaching the backhand. I don't divide the stroke into backswing, hit, and follow-through. I first teach it as the entire swing, having the pupil stand with his right side toward the net. I hold my hand at a point just in front of his right foot and an arm's length away, and tell him to slap my hand with the back of his hand and follow through, stepping toward the net with his right foot at the same time. (Actually, I feel the step is slightly ahead of the swing, but whenever I've tried to teach it that way the pupil is too far ahead and gets nothing from the step.) As the pupil starts to step, his elbow will be bent, his arm close to the body. The slap will straighten his elbow, and his weight will automatically shift forward with the step. The follow-through will turn his hips and shoulders toward the net. This motion approximates the backhand swing and helps the pupil realize how the shot should feel when it is hit correctly.

I show him the backhand grip (turning the hand one-quarter to the left from the Eastern forehand, with the thumb placed diagonally along the handle and with the fingers slightly spread) and then, placing my hand over his, I bounce and hit a few balls with him. Following this, I teach him how to bounce a ball for himself (an almost insurmountable task for some) and hit a backhand. The pupil stands sideways to the net, with the right hand crossed under the left and with the ball in his left hand, palm facing upwards. He has his weight on his right foot and then has to listen to me chant "up" as he tosses the ball a few feet into the air just in front of his right toe, "back" as his weight and racket go back, and "swing and step" as his weight shifts to his front foot and the racket swings through, contacting the ball after it has bounced up waist-high.

Soon I begin tossing balls underhand, starting with my pupil facing me and making him pivot on his left foot, usually screaming at him to keep away from the ball. Almost invariably the beginner (sometimes even the advanced player) hits a backhand with the ball too close to him. After about the tenth consecutive miss, or a clunk on the wood, I stretch his arm and racket to full length to show him what a great reach he has. The right foot stepping toward the ball (I advocate a slightly closed stance) will mean that he must be even further from the ball in order for the elbow to be straightened out at contact. I like the ball hit waist-high or below, which means that I am constantly stressing *keeping well behind the bounce*. The backswing should start "past center" —using center to mean that the racket is stretched out to the back fence. I like a player to have the elbow bent in fairly close to the body at the beginning of the backswing, with the wrist firm; I want to see his racket face slightly open on the straight backswing, *becoming flat at the hit and continuing flat throughout the follow-through*, and I want the finish to be slightly above shoulder height at a point halfway between straight out in front and the right-hand fence.

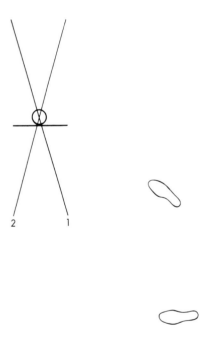

The Backhand Inside-Out Swing.

When the pupil does reasonably well hitting my underhand tosses, I then stand at the net carefully placing balls so that he does not have to move far to get into the right position. At about this stage his arm tightens, the swing shortens, and he says, "I'll never be able to hit a backhand!" Along with

Through the Hitting Area.

Beginning of Inside-Out Swing.

End of Stroke.

standing too close to the ball, the beginner tends to shorten his swing, to point his elbow toward the ball or to drop the racket head and follow through with the face of the racket open.

Eventually (the length of time depends on the capabilities of the pupil), we attempt to rally from the baseline. This rallying is accompanied by more wails from the student, reassurance from me that "you're swinging better, and your judgment will improve with a few thousand more balls hit to the backhand," and frequent forays to the other side of the net to swing with the pupil.

To give some insight into the swing, I frequently draw a large $^1x^2$ on the clay and mark these lines as noted. I tell the pupil to imagine the ball in the center and ask him which line he feels his racket follows before contact. The usual answer is No. 2, and I try to explain that No. 1 is correct. It is the "inside-out theory"—that the right-handed backhand is like a left-handed baseball swing. "Swing from the back," is another expression I use constantly, to try to get across the idea that the swing is a body motion using back, shoulder, and hips.

Some beginners use a two-handed backhand because they feel they haven't the strength to control the shot with one hand. I like to use the left hand on the throat of the racket to pull it into position for the backswing and then to start the racket toward the hit and follow-through. Just before contact I prefer the left hand to drop off, and I feel that the right hand should be strong enough to complete the swing.

Anything that my pupil does correctly, I prefer not to stress. He has enough to think about in simply moving to get into position to hit the ball without thinking of his wrist, backswing, racket face angle, closed stance, pivot, or the position of the racket head. True, he must often be reminded about several of these problems, but if he learns to think of the swing as a whole, he can usually correct one or more defects. If someone asks me, "What is my wrist supposed to be doing?" I have him slap my poor tired hand and find out for himself that there is no excessive wrist action, that the fingers of the hand come around as the racket head should, and that arm, wrist, and racket are almost a straight line at the finish. If he thinks of the hand-slapping or of a throwing and releasing of the racket head, his arm will automatically be relaxed; he will be swinging forward and upward and pivoting his body and shoulders.

Obviously, there will be some shots that cannot be hit with a flat backhand drive. If the ball is at shoulder height or higher, it is extremely difficult to hit the ball flat, and the experienced player will usually chop the ball defensively. I much prefer that the beginner not attempt this until he is grooved with his flat backhand. Otherwise, he will soon be chopping everything in sight. Instead, I keep warning him to stay well behind the bounce so that he can pivot on the back foot and move his weight in with the shot.

There seems to be greater satisfaction for the pupil in finally acquiring a backhand than in learning almost any other shot—perhaps because it appears so impossible to most beginners. A few pupils report that they find the backhand easier than the forehand, but it often turns out that they are natural left-handers. You should definitely expect your students to lag a year or two behind in developing the backhand, but once acquired it may be as strong a weapon as the forehand.

BACKHAND CHECKPOINTS

The Grip:
1. Move one-quarter turn from Eastern forehand.
2. Place thumb diagonally along the handle.
3. Spread fingers slightly.

The Stance:
1. Turn right side toward net.
2. Cross right foot slightly over left toward the left sideline.

The Backswing:
1. Take racket straight back, guided by left hand.
2. Keep arm close to body at end of backswing, elbow bent.
3. Take racket back to "past center," considering center to mean racket stretched out straight to back fence.
4. Have racket face slightly open at end of backswing.

The Forward Swing:
1. Swing the racket inside out and slightly upward.
2. Step with the swing.
3. Straighten arm with the step.
4. Contact ball in front of right foot.
5. Swing from the back—use shoulders, back, and hips.

The Finish of the Swing:
1. Keep arm, wrist, and racket almost in a straight line.
2. End racket slightly above shoulders and pointing halfway between straight out in front and the right-hand fence.
3. Weight should be shifted completely to right foot.

C. Other Techniques

THE BALANCE APPROACH

(Welby Van Horn)

In Part III—the Intermediate, Wayne Sabin describes the "ABC's of Tactics," and his is as clear and precise an explanation of this subject as I have read in a number of years.

Wayne divides tennis into physical, emotional, and intellectual areas, and it is his belief (as it is mine) that "too many players lack an understanding of the significance of the last-named area." He says physical and emotional

Ready Position. Face the net, feet comfortably spread, in a posture of alertness, which enables you to turn equally as quickly for a forehand as for a backhand stroke. Note position of left hand on racket.

Beginning of Backswing. Start of sideways turn of body and feet. Racket leaves left hand.

Start of Forward Swing. Weight is fully on anchor (front) foot. Hips and shoulder begin rotation toward net. This is the beginning of the inside-out swing.

Point of Contact. At this point there is continued rotation of the hips and shoulders, and the beginning of the right foot adjustment to bring you on balance. Note slight rising of right hip ond right shoulder.

End of Backswing. Final sideways turn of body. The balance is similar to that of a tightrope walker.

Left Foot Step and Beginning of Weight Transfer. Left foot makes a 60° angle with the net.

Follow-Through. At the beginning of the follow-through, just after the ball has been contacted, hips and shoulders are facing the net. There is continued adjustment of the right foot, allowing the continuation of hip and shoulder rotation. Right hip and shoulder continue to rise.

End of Stroke. Final adjustment of back foot; hips and shoulders complete rotation. Raising of hips and right shoulder ends.

Ready Position.

Beginning of Backswing. Start of sideways turn of body and feet. Note position of left hand at throat of racket.

Point of Contact. Left hip and left shoulder begin to rise for better forward weight transfer. Note contact point well in front of right foot. Left arm begins to act as a counterbalance.

Follow-Through. Left hip and shoulder continue to rise.

End of Backswing. Final sideways turn of body. Right shoulder is turned slightly away from the net in order to get racket back far enough at completion of backswing.

Start of Forward Swing. Right foot has stepped forward before the beginning of the forward swing. Weight has started to transfer. This is the inside-out swing on the backhand. The right foot forms a 45° angle with the net.

End of Stroke. Final weight transfer to right foot. Raising of left hip and shoulder ends. Note use of left arm for balance.

strength are not enough: One must understand all the basic tactics, the intellectual area of winning tennis. But there are prerequisites to learning all the possibilities in this intellectual area.

While everyone understands the need for teaching basics, I feel that some basics are more important than others. The best formula for sound tennis progress attaches equal importance to four of these basics. Like Wayne Sabin's explanation of tactics, the formula is simple and results in an integrated system of development. It must be followed in this sequence:

1. Balance
2. Grips
3. Strokes
4. Tactics

Balance is the key word. If you start with "tactics" and go backward, you will see what I mean: tactics are of no value unless a player can control the ball; the proper strokes or swing patterns enable him to control the ball; the proper grips enable him to shape a correct swing; the proper balance also enables him to shape this swing, and since balance can be taught and practiced without a racket, it is the prerequisite to the other three basics.

It is impossible for me to overemphasize the importance of balance.

When I am asked, "Why is balance important?" I counter with the question, "Why does the expert make his game (any game requiring movements of the body) look easy?" Of course, it's because he is always on balance. Proper balance means using an economy of motion—it means obtaining the maximum results with a minimum of effort.

Before beginning with an explanation of the balance technique I teach, I will anticipate one question: "Why should we concentrate on these balanced positions when, more often than not, the championship players quite often use different techniques?" Let me explain this as follows.

In championship tennis, the action is so fast that the players seldom have an opportunity to "get set" and assume the proper positions. At this level of play, the player is improvising. To meet the demands of actual play, the championship player must ignore many of the fundamentals that must be used by those of less developed abilities, especially the beginner. Advanced tennis in particular requires "shortcuts"; it demands an improvising technique of hitting off the wrong foot on many occasions, or jumping off the ground with both feet in stroking some fore- and backhand groundstrokes and executing the more difficult volleys. The important thing to remember is this—the championship player could not improvise successfully unless he had devoted many years of training to mastering the fundamentals.

In jazz, improvising is all-important. The musician is playing "off" or "around" a basic melody until it is hardly recognizable. To master this art of improvising, one must be grounded in the fundamentals of music. The championship tennis player is doing the same thing—playing "off" or "around" the fundamentals of balance. Eventually, your pupils will be able to do this also, but they must first master the fundamentals of the forehand and backhand positions of balance as essential to position and footwork.

I must further preface my discussion of the components of sound balance for the forehand and backhand groundstrokes with a brief picture of the footwork I recommend. Balance is applied through sound footwork.

The baseball term "over the plate" describes one dimension of the strike zone. The strike zone in tennis means the correct distance of the ball from the body, especially from the feet. In baseball, the feet are planted, and the ball has to come over the plate; in tennis, the ball is moving, and the feet are planted *at the last moment*. For a comfortable, correct stroke and for best results, a tennis ball should be hit when it is "over the plate."

The greatest fault among beginners and intermediates is a tendency to step too close with the anchor foot (the left foot on the forehand, the right foot on the backhand). This stance is especially common on the forehand and is called the closed stance. Your pupils should not use a closed stance unless, from necessity, they must reach wide for a ball that is not within their strike zone. The correct forehand step with the anchor foot should be forward (toward the net). This is called a square stance. I always refrain from advising the pupil to step into the ball for fear that he will think I want him to step *toward* the ball. One other step is possible with the forehand anchor foot: it is called the open stance, and it should not be practiced by beginners.

I also advocate the square stance on the backhand. Here again, the pupil should take a straight forward step toward the net. This stance is most important in my teaching of balance for both forehand and backhand groundstrokes, because the closed stance will not allow the rotation I teach. I call the rear foot the balance foot; it is used to bring a pupil into balance. I want my pupils to begin and finish their shoulder and hip movement with a back foot adjustment. On the forehand, if the pupil ends up with a closed stance because he must reach for the ball, he makes an extreme adjustment of the right foot, so that at the end of the stroke he is in a square stance. Only with this adjustment can he perform the stroke according to my Balance Approach. Of course, when the square stance is attained at the beginning of either stroke, the adjustment of the rear foot is comparatively minor.

Let's discuss balance on the forehand first, dividing it into eight parts: ready position; beginning of the backswing; final sideways turn of the body; left foot step and weight transfer; start of the forward swing; contact with the ball; beginning of the follow-through; and end of the stroke.

Ready Position. The pupil faces the net, feet comfortably spread, knees bent, weight forward in a posture of alertness and balance that enables him to turn quickly for either a forehand or a backhand. The racket is centered and is held at the throat with the left hand.

Beginning of the Backswing. The body and feet turn sideways. The racket leaves the left hand immediately; the left hand does *not* go back with the racket. This is very important because tennis is a two-arm game. In everything we do, the left arm or hand is always an important balancing element.

Final Sideways Turn of the Body. This is the end of the backswing. In this position, the balance is similar to that of a tightrope walker. The left arm has remained about waist-high.

Left Foot Step and Weight Transfer. The step is straight forward toward the net. The left foot makes a 60° angle with the net. Because the swing goes across the body in the ending, the forehand requires a considerable rotation of hips and shoulders. This is only possible with this 60° turn of the left foot if good balance is to be maintained. The hip as well as the left foot is in a square stance.

Start of the Forward Swing. The weight is fully on the anchor foot. As we are assuming a waist-high ball here, the knee is only slightly bent. On low balls, the pupil will bend his knees and then return to an erect position at the completion of each stroke. This will bring him on balance and enable him to return for the next shot. It is important to see that the pupil does not allow his left foot to slip or turn during the stroke. The 60° angle must be retained throughout the stroke. Only the rear foot turns or adjusts to allow rotation and brings the pupil on balance. It is at the start of the forward swing that the hips and shoulders begin their initial rotation toward the net. This stage also marks the beginning of the inside-out swing.

Contact with the Ball. The hips and shoulders have continued to rotate. It is at this point that the right foot adjustment begins. The right foot pivots; the heel turns to the right. This adjustment of the back foot causes a slight rising of the right hip and shoulder. The head is perpendicular to the swing at this point and should remain fairly stationary and perpendicular to the swing throughout.

Beginning of the Follow-Through. At this point, the hips and shoulders are facing the net. The back foot is continuing to adjust (the foot actually has moved to the right somewhat), allowing the continuation of hip and shoulder rotation. The right hip and shoulder have continued to rise.

End of the Stroke. The final adjustment of the back foot has been made. The hip and shoulder rotation has been completed, along with the rising of the right hip and shoulder. At the end of the stroke, the head is even with the left foot; the right side of the body is slightly higher than the left.

All these principles of balance described for the forehand apply to the backhand. There are only minor differences: the left hand remains at the throat of the racket throughout the backswing, and in the final sideways turn of the body, the right shoulder is turned away from the net to enable the pupil to get his racket back far enough; the right foot makes only a 45° angle to the net. This is because the backhand swing is *away* from the body; therefore, it does not require as much hip and shoulder rotation. The anchor foot provides better balance when placed at only a 45° angle. Because there is less need for hip and shoulder rotation, the amount of the back foot adjustment is less. During contact with the ball, the left hip and left shoulder begin to rise for better forward weight transfer. At this point, the left hand begins to act as a counterbalance. And one last important difference: it will be noted from these descriptions of forehand and backhand balance that the forehand is, basically, more a "shoulder shot" than the backhand is.

If you will study this balance approach carefully, you will observe that through teaching balance, I control the pupil's swing. The length of the backswing, the particular ending I prefer, the degree to which I want a pupil to swing up through the ball—these factors are all determined in good part by the various elements in my concept of proper balance.

THE RHYTHM APPROACH

(*Dennis Van der Meer*)

My system for teaching the groundstrokes is based on two tenets—that tennis should be fun for the pupil from the very start, and that the pupil should never be put in a frustrating situation.

So, I create a rally situation usable from the first lesson. It is, of course, based on the basic principle of the forehand drive. It is also based on another strong belief of mine—that in the beginning the stroke should NOT be taught as a full-length drive (a full-length shot from baseline to baseline). This, in my opinion, is not a usable situation for a beginning pupil for some time, and his ineffectual handling of it can lead to nothing but frustration.

The beginner's ineptness is due to many factors. It takes considerable time for a pupil to develop knowledge of ball behavior, the ability to control his racket, and the ability to move. A ball can rebound at a thousand different heights, speeds, angles, and depths. Two experiments will show you the problem.

First, take your racket back; drop a ball and watch the rebound. Again, take your racket back; drop the ball from the same height, and the instant it touches the ground, close your eyes and swing. Nine out of ten times you will hit the ball. This rebound is predictable; you have seen it before, and you know how to relate it to your racket. But the chances are that a beginner will not be able to do this. His knowledge of rebounds is too limited.

Now, what about the beginner when he is faced with hitting from the baseline? This second experiment clearly gives the answer.

Dip some balls in chalk, or anything that will cause them to leave a mark. From one baseline, aim to the other, trying to hit the same spot with a number of balls. The rebound from the ground should be against a measurable canvas or backboard. If you hit 50 balls you are likely to have 50 marks on the baseline, and the same number on the rebound backboard—there will be only a few duplications. Almost every ball that is hit behaves differently because of human error or inducement (trajectory, speed, and spin). Every player has to build a vast reserve of rebound knowledge and be able to relate this to the racket in order to handle every situation on the court. It will be quite a while before the beginner can effectively handle these varying situations. We want him to hit the ball on the descent, but it will be some time before he can predict where the descent will be. It will be just as long before he develops the ability to move and to control his racket in the full-size stroke required for hitting from baseline to baseline.

Behind my teaching philosophy is a third tenet. I feel that my pupils should know from the beginning that *the size of the stroke is related to the playing situation*; and in future lessons I am always concerned with this principle, and the pupil readily understands me because of the early training. For me, this facilitates the teaching of the volley and the approach shot.

Almost every pupil has a mental picture of the full-length baseline shot. In the very first lesson, I show him that if I want to send a ball a hundred yards, my swing will be much larger than what he thinks is a correct swing. I then demonstrate that if I want to send the ball two feet, my swing would be about an inch and a half long.

But I do believe that a beginner should experience the full-length stroke as early as possible. Even though he won't use it for some time, I want him to feel what it is like to stroke a ball from baseline to baseline. This may take several lessons, of course, but not until we have reached this point will I complicate his life with further advice.

I accomplish this through a controlled progressive situation that includes the following constants: (1) distance of both pupil and instructor from the net; (2) the length of the stroke; (3) the speed and rebound of the ball, and (4) pupil and instructor always doing the same thing.

In the beginning, my pupil and I face each other on opposite sides of the net, two or three yards apart. From here we move back gradually and gradually lengthen the stroke as the distance becomes greater. I feel that the pupil learns very quickly if he has become accustomed to playing the ball back to a predetermined distance and at a predetermined speed; I call this Rhythm Tennis.

Eliminating some of the preliminaries to give you a brief picture of the approach, after we are stationed at the net, we "choke up" our rackets, right up against the throat; we face the net and bounce-tap the ball back and forth across the net, the racket never moving more than a few inches. As our control grows, we move back a few steps, always keeping a correlated distance so that we can hit the ball at the same speed. The swing becomes larger automatically, and we gradually extend our grips toward the handle. The shoulder turn becomes obvious once greater effort is required to send the ball over the net. The stance changes from open to square as we progress. We move back as far as six or eight feet behind the service line, and then work our way forward again. The pupil sees how the size of the stroke becomes reduced. We go back and forth until some control has been established.

I consider some elementary procedures of considerable importance, however. I always begin the lesson by playing catch with my pupil. We catch and toss the ball with our right hands. I want him to see that if he can catch a ball with his right hand, he cannot miss it with a racket as an extension of his hand. I also want him to get used to the word "catch" as a memory peg, so that later when he is using a racket and I ask him to "catch and carry the ball" back to me, he will have the word "catch" well in mind.

Once we are successful at this game of catch, I ask him to hold the racket at the base of the racket head, explaining to him that this makes the racket resemble a large hand; he is to catch the ball on the face of his racket by smothering it with his left hand, then to "ladle" it back to me.

Next, instead of catching the ball on the fly, we let it bounce, catch it and ladle it back. (Remember: I am always doing the same thing the pupil is doing. This provides an example for the pupil to imitate.)

After these preliminaries, we start tapping the ball back and forth to each other, still at close quarters, and I ask him to slide his hand down gradually toward the handle of the racket. I do this to give him the feel of the distance from racket head to ball as early as possible. (I should also note here that when these progressive steps are over, I teach the strokes with the fully extended grip, using the shortened grip for corrective techniques only.) When we start tapping the ball back and forth, I am hopeful that the pupil will recognoize immediately the rebound elasticity of his racket and act accordingly.

We keep one ball going as long as we can and gradually step back until we reach the baseline. Without the pupil's noticing it, the backswing and the follow-through have lengthened, and a decidedly sideways turn has appeared. All of this happens automatically. But, remember, I never get the pupil into a frustrating situation: our ambition is to work back to the baseline on the first lesson, but if we can't get there, we stop at the furthest point at which we can have successful rallies. At this point I will make the pupil aware of how much longer the backswing and follow-through have become and how closely the stroke resembles a full-length drive.

Throughout this progress to the baseline, the pupil is encouraged with the cues, "touch it," "catch it on your racket," "catch and carry the ball," "ladle it back," and "match my speed." Matching my speed is particularly important. If I hit a ball at five miles per hour, I want one back at five miles per hour.

As soon as the pupil reaches the baseline and successfully completes a full-length stroke, I tell him, "See, you can play tennis!" But I temper his elation by explaining that he has been in an extremely controlled situation and that he is not likely to experience success unless it is induced by someone who can control the ball exactly as the situation requires.

This is the point at which the hard work starts, and we will fill in the gaps to make this a functional accomplishment of the pupil, developing stroke technique, knowledge of rebounds, and ability to move. In subsequent lessons, however, I always revert to our original Rhythm Approach.

I now find a rally partner for the pupil and encourage them to work close up inside the service area. This I know they can do successfully now, and they will have fun doing it. They can handle the short swings, and there is little necessity for moving. Most important, the rebound problem is at a minimum. As their skill grows, they will gradually move back. In fact, as a further criterion of levels of play, when the player has reached the stage at which almost every rebound is recognizable and he can handle it through acquired skill, he is well on his way to being an intermediate.

It is always a pleasure to me to see my beginning pupils take my advice and have good rallies from the service line, or to see my intermediate pupils often starting a rally in mid-court and working back slowly. On every level, rhythm is a most important factor in the ability to play the game of tennis. This idea should be instilled from the very beginning.

THE HITTING AREA APPROACH

Sound racket handling in the hitting area is the secret to control on the groundstrokes. One of our most important tasks is to elongate this area by teaching our pupils to carry the ball into court.

The hitting area is the flattened-out portion of the arc that describes a circle or ellipse about the swinger's waist. It begins just behind the ball and continues through point of contact to a foot or more beyond it. A bird's-eye view of this section of the forehand stroke will help you to visualize it.

You will note that the racket comes into the ball in an arc, straightens out as it goes through the ball, and returns to the arc after the follow-through.

Admittedly, this concept of the hitting area places a very confining and unconventional definition on the follow-through—the follow-through lasts only as long as the racket head continues on the intended flight of the ball. On this basis, everything to the left (to the right on the backhand) of the line of flight or follow-through is an ending. The conventional definition of follow-through includes this ending and is frequently stressed at the expense of hitting through the ball. When combined with either turning over or brushing the ball it actually tends to eliminate the follow-through. But the particular ending is not defined, restricted, or specified. Your pupil may end straight out (point to the corner of the fence), or he may end more to the

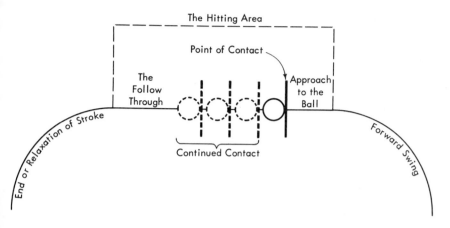

left through a pronounced break in his elbow. Or he may wrap the racket around his neck, and the racket may end flat, open, or closed. It makes little difference as long as the action in the hitting area has been sound; some kind of useful shots (and here we mean variances in spin, trajectory, and speed) will emerge.

This hitting area concept uses the image of a "gun barrel" out of which the pupil "fires the shot." When we use this approach, we are highlighting the three most important parts of the swing: (1) the point of contact, (2) the contact area, and (3) the distance the racket follows the ball on its intended flight.

It is at point of contact, first of all, that shots are made or broken. It is in the follow-through, as we have narrowly defined it, particularly that portion of the follow-through defined as the contact area, that *final* control is obtained, and (equally important) that "feel" and, finally, touch are gained. Everything else in the swing, up to the point of contact, is a preparation for the correct tilt and slant of the racket at point of contact, and long contact with the ball. Everything else after the follow-through is a relaxation of the stroke.

Wayne Sabin calls the point of contact "the moment of truth." He says,

In hitting a tennis ball, the point of impact is the climax. Everything you are doing, from the time a point ends—any physical moves you are making, whether you are walking over to take up position to receive or serve, or taking the racket back and moving into position to hit the ball—everything is taking you toward that point of contact, the moment of truth when the shot is made or butchered. Therefore, all of your physical, mental, and emotional gifts have to be built up to that moment. It is *everything*! As a matter of fact, the thing that is most noticeable about the experienced and competent player is how he does dignify the point of impact, how he does respect it and devote all of his concentration to that instant.

This climactic point is greatly enhanced if the racket stays with the ball for

Racket Lined Up Behind Ball.

Point of Contact.

Follow-Through.

End of Follow-Through.

Racket Lined Up Behind Ball.

Point of Contact.

Follow-Through.

End of Follow-Through.

a long time: if correct balance, weight shift, rotation, and swing allow the hand to direct the racket out on the intended line of flight.

To obtain this long, long look in the hitting area, I repeat, is one of your most important tasks on a tennis court, and it requires the continual use of the cues that will get this effect, such as "hit through the ball," "keep the racket on the ball," "reach out on the ball's flight," "hit the ball for a long time," "stay with the ball," and others. One of the best ways to convey this concept to a pupil is a device Bill Murphy uses: he places six balls in a row on the court and lines his pupils up with the closest ball as point of contact. For the forehand, he explains: "Imagine when you hit the ball that there are six balls connected with each other, and swing the racket through *all six balls* before letting the racket move off to the left."

This action is carrying the ball into the court. This is the contact area.

To amplify this concept, let's inspect what happens at point of contact. When the racket hits the ball, the strings give, the ball compresses, and if ball and racket are moving fast enough, the racket frame bends. These reactions tend to create a "pocketing" effect. The picture of a ball in a La-Crosse stick may be mixing metaphors (since we have said that the hitting area is a gun barrel out of which your pupil fires his shot), but it does provide another image that may help your pupils concentrate on hitting through the ball, carrying it into court.

Very important to this feeling of carrying the ball into court, to going through the hitting area, is the relationship of the wrist to the forearm on the forehand.

Welby Van Horn sets correct wrist action on the forehand through what he calls the "pressed position." This is a specific name, and a good one, for Bill Murphy's "laid back" wrist. Welby says,

> . . . if not exaggerated, the pressed position can be the secret to a sound forehand. It prevents excessive wrist action during the swing. With the pressed wrist, bent elbow and correct shoulder position at the moment of impact with the ball, a pupil has the proper leverage for ball control, and later, power. I regard the pressed position as being similar to a "governor" on a car—a device that prevents speed above a set limit. In this case, the pressed wrist sets a motion speed of the racket hand and prevents over-acceleration and lost ball control through excessive wrist action. For fear of exaggeration, I must warn that the pressed position does not require a fixed, rigid control of the wrist throughout the forehand swing. It can be obtained with a relaxed, but firm, finger grip, and there should be a slight wrist movement in the forehand swing. However, in advanced play, there will be many occasions when it will be impossible to stroke the ball as ideally described. The wrist movement can vary, from slight to moderate to excessive, depending on a multitude of conditions. Like the balance analogy, as the caliber of tennis improves, improvisation is necessary.

Welby has his pupils take this pressed position while they are in ready position. He has them "choke up" the racket grip, holding it at the top of the leather on the handle.

> . . . this serves a twofold purpose: (1) it allows the beginner greater control of the racket during the swing by distributing the weight of the racket more evenly, and (2) it leaves an *extension* of two or three inches—that I use as a guide to a proper stroke. The extension serves as a "built-in" ruler to a good swing. If the pupil makes his forehand backswing and follow-through correctly, the extension will be separated from the inside (lower part) of the wrist. This prevents a wrist collapse, and the collapse is most often the greatest single groundstroke problem, both forehand and backhand, the beginner and many intermediates face.

Wrist collapse includes dropping the racket head as well as an excessive forward action of the wrist. Van Horn considers the pressed wrist position one of the secrets of feel and touch on the forehand. It is interesting to note that Bill Murphy's "six balls exercise" requires this pressed wrist position.

Stress has been on the forehand particularly here because most pupils have a more difficult time staying with the ball on the forehand than they do on the backhand. The hitting area is of equal importance on the backhand, however.

The racket action in the hitting area is affected by all of the mechanics of the stroke, the dynamics, and the other basics. The use of this approach as a full-blown teaching technique requires the relating of all of these factors to the hitting area.

Footwork and Position. Unless proper position is obtained—a comfortable arm's length from the ball—it is impossible to get sound action in the hitting area. The player who is too close to the ball must use a different kind of stroke. He will be forced to push rather than swing through the ball; standing too far away is even more detrimental to sound racket action on the ball. The skip steps you will teach your Beginner will simplify the problem of position and provide a proper base for sound action in the hitting area.

Inside-Out Swing. This is a very important part of the shaping of the strokes. It is the first arc in our hitting area diagram. There are many cues for teaching it—"swing the racket toward the right, or left, net post" (for the forehand and backhand, respectively), "swing from inside the line of flight to the outside," "swing from the inside to the outside of the ball" (the inside of the ball is toward the pupil). The elbow moves from relatively close to the body to farther away. Pauline Addie's $^1x^2$, as explained in her chapter on the backhand, is the best presentation I have seen to convey the inside-out swing concept. (The inside-out swing is line 1 on the backhand, line 2 on the forehand as the pupil stands behind the drawn X.)

Rotation. Proper rotation implies a smooth, gradual turning of hips and shoulders into the shot, so that the racket can be placed on the ball at a right angle to the intended line of flight and so that the racket will be going out on the intended line of flight. On the forehand, the pupil will be approximately facing the ball when he contacts it. The right shoulder, however, will be slightly behind the playing arm, the pressed wrist will establish a 45° angle between the forearm and racket shaft. On the backhand, the shoulders will approximate a right angle to the net; the playing arm and racket will form an approximately straight line.

Weight Shift. A good weight shift further assures elongation of the hitting area. It is important that the stance be a broad one and that the feet be placed in a square stance for the forehand and square or slightly closed for the backhand. One of the reasons for good footwork is to obtain a sound base for shifting the weight.

In using this approach, as Bill Murphy says, "We continually stress the importance of proper stance, weight shift, rotation, and balance to the hitting area, showing how it's easier to hit the ball for a long time if one pivots, shifts his weight, and so forth." Also, we relate the dynamics of our basic concept of ball control and all the mechanics to this area.

Let's end this discussion with sound advice from Welby Van Horn.

> Above all, I try to instill mental discipline by overcoming the almost irresistible urge to hit a tennis ball too hard. It is essential to refrain from this temptation, to remember always that you "stroke" a ball over the net—not hit, block, smash, or drive it. When you "stroke," you are swinging with thought and applying a sense of feel coming from the fingertips. And you can evaluate each stroke by the feel and the sound. There is more of a similarity between a tennis racket and a stringed instrument than just the strings. Anyone can improve his game by listening to the ball as well as watching it.
>
> A sense of feel coming from the fingertips—and it is, after all, the hand and only the hand that swings the racket into the ball, that transfers all the energy into the Hitting Area. Thus in working for control in this section, we are continually trying to transmit to our pupils the feeling for contact that is transferred to the ball through the fingers.

D. Watching the Ball

Concentration on the ball is a must. It is the key to watching it, of course. All of us use the term, "watch the ball," but often we use it as a crutch, a substitute for telling pupils *how* to watch the ball, what it really means and how to relate the ball to the racket.

If off-center hitting is a problem, it may help if we explain the difference between *watching* the ball and merely *seeing* it as a white blob somewhere out there in space.

Try it this way: Set your pupil up with his racket back, and mark an X on the court. Hold the ball on the X and tell him that you are going to carry the ball in your hand from the X to him. He is to hit it with the *center* of the racket, *but he must keep his eyes fixed on the X mark.* When you do this, he will hit it off-center, probably somewhere on the wood, because of course he is not looking *at* the ball. At this point, while he is looking at the X, ask him if he can see the ball out of the corner of his eye. He will be able to, and you can explain to him that this is what you mean by seeing it but *not* watching it. Then go through the same process, this time allowing him to watch the ball as you bring it into the hitting area. He will find it easy to hit it in the center of his racket.

Here is another gimmick that combines watching the ball with some of the basics—a simple way to explain their relationship to beginners. This is the Back-Bounce-Hit trick. When teaching the forehand, you can explain this cue to your pupil this way: "The very second the ball leaves my racket and you have determined direction, I want you to say 'Back' to yourself, and act on it. Take the racket back as you give yourself the command. Now, watch the ball come over the net and down into the bounce; when it bounces, say 'Bounce' (not just before or just after the bounce, but *right at the point at which the ball bounces*). When you are ready to hit the ball, swing in and say 'Hit' at point of contact, about two inches in front of your left foot. Back-Bounce-Hit."

In most cases this will improve your pupil's hitting immediately. If it doesn't, ask him to say the "Back-Bounce-Hit" *aloud*. You will find that he is either saying "Back" too late, or "Bounce" too late or too early, which will throw him off his timing on the all-important "Hit" command. He may be precise on the "Back" and the "Bounce" but saying "Hit" too early or too late. (And don't be surprised, either, if you find that he has been saying "Bounce-Back-Hit.") At any rate, the necessary corrections will set him straight.

It is obvious that this device embraces much more than eye control. It sharpens reactions and concentration. It accentuates the early backswing; it stresses *an awareness of the ball as something that must be followed from racket to racket* and must be reacted to the minute it leaves an opponent's racket; it also helps a pupil to measure the beat of the ball. A fast ball will be "Back-Bounce-Hit." A slow ball will be "Back- - -Bounce- - -Hit." This method will improve his rhythm and his timing and will, therefore, be an aid to direction or placement.

In addition, it may help him to highlight the hitting area, to keep his racket on the ball longer. When all the usual expressions fail to get this result, I have found that there is something about the unconscious reaction to saying "Hit" at point of contact that makes the racket follow the ball over a longer path.

Here is another important tip to the pupil when you are working on the problem of watching the ball: *keep a steady head*! Welby Van Horn explains it this way,

In golf, it is absolutely necessary to keep your head steady during the swing. I think this reminder is equally important in tennis. I feel that keeping the head steady is an assist in *how to watch the ball*. This is how I explain its importance: "Imagine that you have a glass of water on top of your head as you swing slowly, and try not to spill the water. Certainly, you must move your head to watch the ball go back and forth from your opponent's racket to yours, but it is often a violent jerking or bobbing of the head at point of impact with the ball which prevents many players from watching the ball. By not controlling your head during the swing, you divert your eyes from the ball and destroy your timing. A downward thrust of the head near the moment of impact with the ball is also the main reason why beginners get too close to the ball and hit it on the throat of the racket. Try keeping your head steady on the groundstrokes, and I think you will be amazed at the results; you will find yourself hitting a majority of the balls in the exact center of the strings."

And here are some cues from Dennis Van der Meer that relate the use of the racket to the ball: "Put the ball in the center of your racket"; "send your racket out to collide with the ball."

It is amusing to think that such a basic thing as watching the ball could be a controversy in tennis, but it is; mostly in terms of the extent to which pupils need reminders. Here again, as in everything else, the necessity for reminders depends on the individual pupil. Many will require few warnings and little explanation, but with others the unpleasant sound of wood will exhaust the imagination of the teacher.

E. Moving For the Ball

Let's talk about footwork for a minute, from two divergent points of view—one, that of a teacher who rarely talks about footwork; the other, that of a purist on the subject.

Now just what makes the first one tick? Imagine rarely talking about footwork, the very crux of the game! Well, he just might believe that footwork is something that comes naturally; perhaps most of the pupils he has seen have had some kind of game experience, if no more than tossing balls back and forth. Possibly he even started them with paddles at a Ping-Pong table. Or he might believe that footwork should be natural, that there are a good many different stances for hitting forehands and backhands. Or he might say that he could induce good footwork naturally, through corrective techniques like having a pupil face the net and hit balls for a few minutes because he was continually crossing the left foot over the right foot when he hit a forehand. (He might even have an open mind about open footwork!) Finally, he might tell us this: "I believe the behavior of the playing arm is far more important than the way the feet behave. I believe that all my pupils are going to end up hitting the ball with their feet sideways, crisscrossed, backwards, and forwards, so I'm going to concentrate on racket handling and teach them the flexibility they need to control the ball, rather than worry them about their feet."

Now what of our purist? He might tell us that "the purpose of good footwork is to move the playing arm into the right position to make a balanced stroke. Good footwork is a balanced base that allows proper rotation and weight shift—freedom of swing."

The purist, of course, would be very rigid in his beliefs, full of proper ways to move for the ball, and very precise about stance. Perhaps he arrived at his point of view because he feels that good footwork comes first, arm action second. In fact, he might say that without proper footwork, sound arm action is impossible; or footwork might be the basis of his view of balance or weight shift or rotation.

Two very divergent views of the importance of footwork, aren't they? And which is the better teacher of this particular phase of the game? I like them both. Each may have something to offer the other, but I'd never question the fact that each of them could turn out good players. In spite of our liberal's point of view, we do need some "tags" (to identify the work of the feet), and we need to present a picture of stance and of moving.

Ordinarily, the position foot is the name we give the right foot on hitting the forehand, the left foot on hitting the backhand. We talk about them in terms of position steps. We call them anchor feet, too. The hitting foot is the opposite for each stroke. The hitting step, we say, but some of us will call the left foot (when hitting the forehand) or the right foot (when hitting the backhand) adjustment steps, as we will see later. Van Horn calls the front foot the anchor foot, the rear one the balance, or adjustment, foot. These terms express most precisely his concept of balance in footwork.

Now, let's make a couple of nice safe statements about stance:

(1) We want a pupil to be the right distance from the ball (a comfortable distance, with the elbow slightly bent on both sides at point of contact); a straight arm is the preference of many on the backhand.

(2) We want a pupil to be the right distance from the bounce of the ball.

On the forehand, most teachers agree that the ideal stance for beginners is the square one (the feet are on a line perpendicular to the net); this is the stance that allows maximum weight shift and the proper rotation or pivot, but a slightly closed stance (the left foot slightly across the right toward the right sideline) is not harmful. However, much of tennis literature has suggested the very closed stance on the forehand, and this can be termed incorrect. This is a stance we would want a pupil to use only when absolutely necessary, because it curtails rotation and weight shift and therefore, racket action in the hitting area. It is interesting to see how Van Horn avoids this extremely closed stance for his pupils with his balance foot adjustment. So, a *slightly* closed stance is within our range of correctness on the forehand. However, the slightly *open* stance (the left foot closer to the left sideline than the right foot) is somewhat controversial. Van Horn believes that this stance should be used by the advanced player only. On the other hand, Chet Murphy and I both teach it as a means for the beginner to get away from the close ball. Probably the thinking of most teachers would coincide with Van Horn's.

When hitting a backhand, a slightly closed stance is the most acceptable one. The pupil needs more shoulder-turn here to get the racket back. A square stance is acceptable, however, and the open stance should be avoided for the beginner.

One final point on stance: the difference between the angle placement of the front foot on the backhand and on the forehand in the Van Horn Balance Approach is most important—60° for the forehand, 45° for the backhand.

Most important for beginners is our second statement on stance: "We want a pupil to be the right distance from the bounce of the ball." Welby Van Horn defines the *right* distance most succinctly,

> My teaching of the forehand and backhand demands, in the beginning, hitting the ball "on the descent" as it reaches the approximate level of the waistline, or slightly below the waistline. I use a method of counting to determine the correct timing—the exact moment the ball is stroked. It involves the use of these numbers—one, two, three. Count "one" when your opponent hits the ball; count "two" when the ball bounces on your side of the court; count "three" when you stroke the ball. If performed exactly as described, the significance of the counting is such that at the moment you stroke the ball (three), your counting will be in an even tempo. An even tempo will necessitate going back for deep balls, and up for short ones, and the ball will always be contacted waist-high.

Now what about moving for the ball? All this talk about stance must be tied in with moving for the ball. Pupils can't be spoon-fed forever. Obviously, if the ball is close, only a pivot is needed. If it is some distance away, two methods are acceptable—running or skipping.

At the proper time, it's important to introduce "skip steps" to the beginner. Many of us will do this as soon as he is hitting satisfactorily from a stationary position.

Skip steps can be difficult to teach and difficult to learn, and they are even more difficult to put on paper. To see them clearly, visualize a boxer moving from left to right or a basketball player guarding his man. The technique is this: when a player is hitting the forehand, the right foot goes out first, then the left foot is brought up to the heel of the right foot as the player skips off his right foot; when he is hitting the backhand, the left foot moves first. Close balls require only one of these skips; balls some distance away require two or three. If the ball is further away than this, they cannot be used; he must run for the ball.

As a player moves into position with this footwork, his shoulders turn and the racket goes back in preparation for the hit. When his right foot is positioned for the ball, he steps with his left foot to match the bounce. If he is too close to the ball, he assumes an open stance; if he has positioned himself correctly, he assumes a square stance. If he is not close enough to the ball, he will use a slightly closed stance. On the backhand, his right foot will move into a slightly closed or square stance, dependent on his position from the ball. Again, open footwork should be avoided here because it hinders the shoulder-turn.

It helps to emphasize Bill Murphy's term, "the early, unhurried backswing," with this footwork. The racket starts back the instant the right foot moves out on the forehand. The shoulders turn; the racket goes back; the foot goes out, all at the same time—as if there were a rod attached from the throat of the racket to the right foot. This tie-in helps to build *instant preparation*, which is essential to the successful execution of a stroke. The skip steps are worthless if your pupil skips out, facing the net, and upon arrival at the ball decides that this is a good time to be thinking about getting his racket back. Actually, he should be coiling into a "shoulders perpendicular to the net" position as his feet skip out parallel to the net on the forehand, into a somewhat more closed shoulder position on the backhand. The racket *must* be at the end of the backswing when he is ready to take the hitting step.

Delaying the hitting step is important for more than just an adjustment to the bounce, however. The step is made after the bounce because of the timing and rhythm of the stroke. Chet Murphy says, "When tossing balls from close up, I time their step and hit, by having them use a rhythm that goes like this: bounce– – –step-hit, with a pause after the bounce, and the step-hit close together. I find it helps the beginner to learn to step in relation to the swing."

Because the skip steps are not easy for everyone to acquire, I feel it is best to start early in teaching them. In the beginning, have your pupils practice skip steps without balls and racket. They will stumble over the steps for a bit because they will seem unnatural. When you begin to hit balls to them, be certain they do not have to use more than one of these skips to attain position.

Now that we have gotten them into hitting position, they must get back (return to court position). The moves for this are very definite: on the forehand, the left foot is the first step back toward the center of the court; on the backhand, the right foot. And then the skip steps begin again. They are most important on the return.

Skip steps should also be used on all deep balls. The pupil merely turns sideways to the net and then starts his skip steps backwards. They are also useful on short balls that are close, when only one skip step is necessary.

Well, we've come a long way from our antifootwork friend, haven't we? And what about him? Perhaps if he reads this at all, he'll recognize a few tags, a few stances, a bit of footwork he's seen before and used.

In fact, he might brush us off this way, "Yes, I know all that! You haven't told me anything new. Isn't the main point here that different pupils need special kinds of footwork attention for various reasons—become they're too close to the ball, run past the ball, are awkward and stiff, or show 'unrhythm' in their moving? Isn't the attention we need to give to footwork, like watching the ball, dependent on each pupil?"

F. The Mechanics and Corrective Techniques

Tennis is an easy game to play. All we need to tell pupils is to watch the ball, get the racket back early, and hit the ball where their opponent isn't or where he doesn't like it. Very simple. To paint a Mona Lisa, first draw a face! But how many faces before you get the right face? How many corrections before ball control is firmly implanted?

What we are teaching on the groundstrokes can be summed up briefly— *let the racket head do the work*. We want pupils to have a firm (but not tight) grip on the racket and to *swing* it. We want them, simply, to learn to control the racket through their fingers, to let the racket head do the work. However, it often takes considerable explanation and time to unravel the various complications before the concept is fully grasped. And so, more frequently than not, our ideal of teaching the whole swing is tossed right out the window as we see mistakes in the use of elbows, wrists, shoulders, footwork, and so on.

We need to use "corrective techniques," as Dennis Van der Meer phrases it, to straighten out these various complications. This implies a knowledge of the mechanics in depth.

We have already presented to you a number of corrective techniques, but not as such; they were presented as devices for teaching the swing—for instance, Van Horn's "choked-up racket," Pauline Betz Addie's "X," Murphy's "six balls trick," the use of a wall or a fence. All these ideas can be used as corrective techniques.

This discussion of the mechanics will provide a few more examples for you. For this purpose, let's break down the backhand and forehand swings into four parts: (1) the backswing; (2) the forward swing; (3) point of contact, and (4) follow-through (conventional definition) and ending.

THE BACKSWING

Here are three important points for both the forehand and backhand backswing: it should be early, simple, and short.

Be sure your pupil is always starting the racket back when you hit or toss the ball. Remember, starting early is the key to avoiding that frenzied hurrying; the late, hurried backswing causes a bookful of ills on both backhand and forehand. The answer here is an early turn of the shoulders.

As Chet Murphy says, "Once I get that early turn of the shoulders set, I am confident that the backswing is on its way."

Welby Van Horn describes the backswing this way: "The shoulders turn, bringing the racket back about to the right hip. The backswing starts here."

You have noted in earlier chapters that Bill Murphy and Pauline Betz Addie have discussed two different types of backswing: Bill's is circular; Pauline's is straight back. This is purely a matter of style, and a choice between styles is mainly a teacher's personal preference. Many teachers prefer to start all beginners with a straight backswing. There is nothing "wrong" with this; it's simpler, possibly. When working with a pupil who has had some experience playing the game and has developed or been taught a stiff, full-armed, straight backswing, sometimes the suggestion of making a slight circle will help to break the stiffness. Conversely, if a pupil wiggles the racket all over the place on the backswing, or takes it back with an elbow somewhere out in space, or with a collapsed wrist, a straight backswing will often give him more control over the two racket edges. To repeat our point, one of the basic things we are working on with beginners is finger control over those two edges, so that the pupil feels exactly where they are at point of contact.

Chet Murphy says,

I try to teach my pupils the preparatory movements which will enable them to obtain the proper relationship of the racket to the ball at point of contact. That's why I teach the kind of backswing I do—straight back from the waiting position, (not necessarily, however, with the racket handle level or parallel to the ground). In the waiting position, the pupil supports the racket at the throat with his left hand. Normally, the racket slants upward a little and is positioned just above waist height. Then the pupil turns sideways about 90°—turns both body and feet. He does nothing else; in other words, the left hand still supports the racket at the throat. With this single movement your pupil has already made half of his backswing. Now he releases the left hand and carries the racket back another 90° to 110°, raising or lowering the racket, dependent on the height of the ball. He is now ready for the forward swing.

This is a good picture to help eliminate all the arm waving and overwork that goes into a beginner's backswing. It is an excellent image to portray control over the two racket edges. Also, it shows the importance of the shoulder-turn in the backswing.

Whenever a pupil overswings on the backswing, I stress the shoulder-turn as a corrective technique, to show how little arm action is needed on the backswing if the proper shoulder-turn is made.

If a pupil's backswing is causing trouble, I toss or hit balls to him as he stands *with his racket already back.* This technique is a bit artificial, granted, but teaching beginners requires "gimmicks" at times.

Generally, we think of the racket as flat in the backswing on the forehand and going back slightly open on the backhand because the forearm rotates as we take the racket back on the backhand side. However, many teachers teach a slightly closed face, some a slightly open face, on the forehand. Neither is outside our range of correctness, certainly. A closed face on the backhand *is*, however, very definitely! What's important here is how the racket looks at the end of the backswing on both sides.

Teach a short backswing as well as an early, simple one. Using a wall and a clock as guides, Bill Murphy recommends that the racket touch the wall at seven o'clock when the pupil stands a foot from it. Welby Van Horn uses the wall approach with the pupil one foot from the wall and suggests that at the end of the backswing, the racket should be a foot from the wall, also, at six o'clock. Even five o'clock is permissible. On the backhand, any position from six o'clock to four o'clock would be within a range of correctness.

To a large extent, the distance on the backswing depends upon the degree of shoulder-turn that you teach. Generally speaking, on the forehand the shoulders form a perpendicular to the net at the end of the backswing; they form approximately a 30°–45° angle to the net on the backhand.

Undoubtedly, overswinging is one of the most common faults in beginners. Welby expresses the relationship of the length of the backswing to the forward swing this way:

If you divide the total length of the forehand swing into two parts from the end of the backswing to the end of the follow-through, and use the center of the body (standing sideways to the net) as a division point, one-third of the total swing length would be used for the backswing and two-thirds for the forward swing and the follow-through. This should not be too difficult to understand, but it is difficult to put into practice. The majority of beginners and intermediates feel they will not develop sufficient power with the shorter backswing, so we must continually point out the *unimportance of power at this point*, and show them how an excessive backswing leads to many of the forehand ills, such as hitting on the wood, hitting too late, poor balance and a general loss of control over the racket face.

The relationship and the cautionary note are applicable to the backhand, also.

An important point to consider is the relationship of the elbow to the body at the end of the backswing. The arm is bent at the end of the backswing on both sides. On the backhand, the elbow should be fairly close to the body and almost at midwaist; on the forehand, it should be a short distance away from the body.

As a corrective technique for a "straight arm" at the end of the forehand backswing, Chet Murphy suggests this:

Place a ball under the pupil's right arm (in the armpit); have him lower the arm toward his body to pinch or squeeze the ball. Then have him lift or raise the forearm and the hand and racket so that they are parallel to the ground. The elbow is now close to the body, close enough to keep the ball in the armpit. If the pupil will stroke tossed balls that bounce waist-high, it will automatically teach him to keep his elbow bent.

I stress the fact that when hitting or tossing balls to a pupil, I do not want to see the racket at the end of the backswing on the forehand side, and I barely want to see it on the backhand side.

We want a concentrated backswing, and so we will try to eliminate all extraneous movements of the racket in this phase of the swing. On the forehand, for example, Van Horn suggests this idea, "Imagine in the backswing that you have a nickel on the top edge of your racket, and then try to take the racket back to the end of the backswing without allowing the nickel to drop off." We want a controlled ending, too, and will work to get this desired effect. However, there are some lessons in which a pupil will not be able to respond to a suggested muscular pattern change; for example, the elimination of a wiggle in the forehand backswing. It is sound teaching, then to drop this approach and work on the hitting area or the ending. Perhaps progress can be made in eliminating the backswing difficulty in the next lesson.

In addition to all of these details on the backswing, keep in mind that we want our pupils to *measure* the ball with the backswing. The preparation is higher for the high ball, lower for the low ball. Just as important as control over the racket face is the relationship of the racket at the end of the backswing to point of contact. We want the racket slightly below the waist-high ball, somewhat lower on the low ball and either above or *well* below the high ball, depending on whether they are going to hit down on it or up over it.

This may seem like overattention to a backswing, but all of it is necessary if the pupil is going to have the racket ready and right for a sound forward swing, for sound action in the hitting area.

THE FORWARD SWING

Wayne Sabin says of the forward swing, "I believe the best way to shape the strokes on both sides is to 'create a wall' with the face of the racket by keeping it approximately perpendicular to the court surface and come through with the racket perpendicular from beginning to end." (It will go from open to flat on the backhand.)

As a corrective technique to set the proper forward swing, Bill Murphy uses the ball-under-the-arm trick: "The ball should be kept in place almost halfway through the forward swing, and it should fall to the ground as the elbow moves away from the body, striking the ground close to the player's left toe."

Some teachers allow beginners to hit a two-handed backhand, perhaps thinking that the pupil does not have the necessary strength to hit with one hand. This is permissible only if a teacher really knows what he is about and can eventually get that left hand off the racket at the end of the backswing. Use of the left hand on the forward swing can be a bad influence in terms of rotation, balance, and the basic principle of swinging the racket head. I believe the left hand does *nothing* but leave the racket at the end of the backswing. It does *not* take the racket back; it does *not* push it forward. The left hand on the racket is like Linus's blanket. It gives the pupil a nice feeling for where the racket is and gives him something to do with the left arm. It is my opinion that overuse of the left hand can cause as much trouble on the backhand as any other factor. Frequently I will suggest that a pupil practice the backhand with the left hand off the racket to help him get the feel of swinging the racket and letting the racket head do the work. If he likes it this way, I suggest that he never put it back on again. If the left hand *is* used, however, two choices are permissible: the pupil can let it remain at the throat throughout the backswing, or he can slide the racket through the fingers so that both hands are close together at the end of the backswing.

POINT OF CONTACT

Now we enter an area of discussion that I have been avoiding so far: two variations from our basic concept of control. We have stated that we want to see a slightly upward swing with a flat racket at contact and throughout the follow-through. With the following deviations—slightly open racket face on low balls and slightly closed on high balls if we teach him to "throw" his racket up over the ball on high backhands and forehands—this is safe ground. We have said that we do not want the pupil consciously to turn the racket over the ball. However, if a pupil has a natural rotation of the forearm through the follow-through, he would be within our range of correctness. The racket would end, then, not "on edge" or flat, but slightly closed. This is "covering" the ball, and it does provide a further "sealing" of the flight of the ball. However, most of us are adamant about not allowing the top edge to come over on the backhand. There is a tendency to teach the backhand as an open-face shot. Many consider this the most natural way to hit a backhand, and the safest. The face is open at contact and remains open in the follow-through. It is *slightly* open, or flat at the end of the shot. The basic concept of a slightly upward swing remains intact here, and so we end up with an open-face shot that has some topspin. We are still discussing the drive; the open face is mainly used with the waist-high and lower balls, however.

All these variations may emerge out of the natural tendencies of your pupils. If it is natural for them to cover the ball on their forehand, let them: if they control the ball better with an open-face backhand, let them. If you understand and teach the groundstrokes better this way, do so.

A further word about direction: we said the basic point was point of contact. This may vary: a pupil will hit earlier for the cross-court shot and later for the down-the-line shot than he would for the straight-ahead shot. We can also include the slant of the racket and the direction of the swing as factors of importance. Lining the feet up in the direction of the flight of the ball is commonly considered one of the ways to get direction, but most of us would disagree with this.

Another point about the position of the body (on the forehand and backhand) at point of contact: on the forehand, the body is not sideways; it is considerably open in relation to the net. On the backhand, however, overrotation will limit the racket action in the hitting area, causing the racket to come across the line of flight. At contact, the position of the shoulders should be from slightly open to perpendicular to the net.

FOLLOW-THROUGH AND ENDING

We need to add only one point here to what has already been said, but it is a most vital one, as it concerns the acquisition of touch. "Touch," Van Horn says, "can be acquired by the beginner and intermediate by swinging in *slow motion*, especially as it pertains to the follow-through of the groundstrokes. The swing should be brought to a gradual stop. If the hips turn, the right shoulder is used, and the right foot brings the pupil on balance, he should be able to complete his swing so that the ending coincides with the bounce of the ball as it strikes the opposite side of the court. If he has a clearance of three or four feet over the net with the ball, he will have more time to complete his swing in this manner and then get ready for the next return.

This easy swing, gradually slowing down, will help pupils to feel the ball in the hitting area.

Quite frequently, there is one simple (but troublesome) cause for many of the mechanical difficulties—tension. And so we tell pupils there are two places to be firm in tennis, the hand and the head; that the swinging parts— the arm and the shoulder—must be relaxed, because they can't swing the racket if they are not relaxed.

Finally, they get the idea. Maybe it's that one good shot when they didn't overwork, didn't even try to hit the ball, it seemed; when they let the racket head do the work for them. Now they are on the road to ball control and to hitting the ball where their opponent isn't or where he doesn't like a ball to be hit.

Probably we won't "draw the right face" for quite a while, but a good many corrections later (not all of them on the same pupil, I hope!), a few faint smiles should begin to show if we successfully use a bit of corrective craftsmanship.

A. The Serve

(*Welby Van Horn*)

The serve, of all the strokes in tennis, is the easiest to teach and to learn. It is the most difficult stroke to *perfect*. The final shaping of this stroke as used by championship players bears little resemblance to the initial shaping of the stroke that beginners should use. For this reason alone, the separation of the serve stroke into three chapters (for beginners, intermediates, and advanced players) is necessary and important in order to guide instructors and pupils properly through the development of the serve. Remember, the basic idea throughout this book is progression, which is a new idea in tennis instruction. This is, in my opinion, a revolutionary approach, and I believe that excellent results will be obtained if you follow the guidelines carefully.

To set the stage for the beginners' service, some general discussion is necessary. First, it is important to repeat the instructional formula of fundamentals which I have found to be the most successful. The formula applies to the serve as well as to the forehand and backhand. It includes, in order: (1) the balance, (2) the grips, (3) the stroke (shaping of the swing), (4) the intelligent use of the serve. In addition, the teaching of the serve includes a fifth element—the toss of the ball.

Each fundamental within this formula, along with the fifth element, should change shape as instruction progresses from one level to the next. This is why the serve is difficult to perfect!

Together, the fundamentals of the formula, as well as the fifth element, form a cohesive combination of five factors at *each* stage of development. For example: in the initial development, the average beginner should not attempt to use the grip

SHAPING THE SERVE, THE VOLLEY, AND THE LOB

of an advanced player, just as an advanced player would not use a beginner's grip. Further, certain key movements in the swing, weight distribution, and balance will be altered as progress continues—so much so, in fact, that the final shaping of all the elements is not anything like these elements used by a beginner. Yes, even the seemingly simple toss of the ball will change. The direction of the toss is *directly* related to all these key movements, and especially to the grip being used. Like a sculptor who starts with a mass of clay or similar material, the instructor should shape the elements gradually and meticulously toward the final classical service motion.

Let's emphasize again that the serve is the easiest stroke to teach and the easiest to learn, for these reasons:

1. Unlike the forehand and backhand, the service stroke allows ample time to prepare. (You can be deliberate in placing your feet and body and in getting your grip. You have reasonable time mentally to shape your swing and balance before the actual execution. *Concentration* is the key word.)
2. Unlike the forehand and backhand, the serve gives you, *not* your opponent, control of the ball. (In this instance, control of the ball means using the correct toss in regard to height and direction. In serving, you should not "chase" the ball, and you won't if your toss is correct.)
3. Unlike the forehand and the backhand, the serve is the only stroke in tennis a player can begin and then stop before completing (after a poor toss). It is vitally important to recognize a poor toss, and doing so requires concentration. Far too many beginners do not have the concentration or discipline to stop their swings. Unfortunately, stopping the swing until a correct toss is made is disconcerting to an opponent in a match or even in a friendly game.
4. More than any other stroke, the serve can best be practiced alone. (You do not need an opponent to master the fundamentals of my formula, or the fifth element, the toss of the ball.)

For these reasons I feel the serve is easy to learn. An additional reason is the similarity of the service motion (swing) to that of the overhanded throwing motion as used by baseball players. Many instructors, in fact, use the term, "throwing the racket at the ball," but the beginner must be warned not to throw the racket at a poorly tossed ball.

Initially, the mechanics of the beginner's serve should be combined in a simple motion without frills. The beginner should never attempt to copy the more complex movements of the championship player.

We are ready now for your first lesson in teaching the serve.

BALANCE

This is the first consideration in my formula of teaching. It is the most important fundamental. However, before balance is explained, the starting

Stance.

Down.

Back.

Up.

Toss.

Hit.

Balance.

stance must be covered briefly. See that your pupil assumes the following stance:

1. The left foot should be at a 45° angle to the baseline, from two to four inches behind the line.
2. The right foot should be parallel to the baseline, feet spread at approximately the width of the shoulders and toes and heels touching two imaginary lines that run at a right angle to the baseline.
3. The weight should rest slightly on the right foot, which will raise the heel of the anchor foot (left foot) approximately one inch from the ground.
4. Hips and shoulders must be sideways to the net.

Once the pupil has assumed the proper stance, we are ready to teach him balance.

Actually, the only difference between the service balance and the forehand balance is the beginning stance. On the forehand, you begin from a stance facing the net (the ready position); on the serve, you begin from a sideways position. All of the other movements in the rotation of the hips, shoulders, adjustment of the back foot to allow the rotation, and weight distribution from back to forward foot are the same. The pupil should not step forward with the anchor (left) foot, as he would on the forehand. Thus the left foot really does constitute an anchor.

The chain of events that occur in balance is really quite simple. The back foot makes an adjustment in order to allow the hip and shoulder rotation. The hip and shoulder rotation allows a complete and free follow-through of the stroke in an on-balance position.

A very important factor in the balance I teach on the serve is that the beginner must *not* bring his right foot over the baseline. (He is often trying to copy the more advanced player.) More often than not, the beginner moves over the baseline because he is chasing a ball he has tossed too far in front or to the side. He also equates this extreme forward movement with more power. Once again, *the beginner is not after power.* He should concentrate on a proper toss, control of the body through balance, and hitting the ball easily. A proper toss will enable the beginner to assume the basic balanced position *after the stroke is completed.* In addition, the beginner may make the mistake of falling over the baseline when serving or chasing a poor toss.

GRIP

Generally speaking, beginners will develop a more useful serve if they start with a grip somewhere between the Eastern grip and the Western grip. This type of grip allows the beginner to get more of the racket on the ball at the moment of contact. He will, of course, be hitting a fairly flat ball with this grip, and this is consistent with the basic premise behind our teaching of the groundstrokes in this book that the beginner should not be taught spin shots. In my opinion, it is a mistake to teach the average beginner even a forehand grip, which is still short of the grip used by championship players. The position of your fingers in the grip should, starting from the little finger, read: finger, finger, finger, thumb (around the handle), finger. This grip should not change materially until considerable time has been spent on perfecting the balance and swing shape (stroke). The finger relationship of the grip will never change.

In my teaching of the serve, *where* the racket is held is just as important as *how.* I have the pupil "choke up" on the handle so that there will be about a three-inch extension of the handle below the grip. If this extension hits his arm during the swing, his wrist motion in throwing the racket at the ball has been incorrect. As in my teaching of the forehand and backhand, this extension serves as a guide to a proper swing.

STROKE

When the player has practiced his balance (I suggest that he use a mirror for this purpose) and knows his grip, he is ready to begin the serve stroke. Actually, it is not a stroke in the sense we use this word for "feeling" the forehand and backhand groundstrokes and volleys. Rather, the beginner will use a slight pushing motion (which comes from the grip being used at this level of play) instead of a pulling motion, which comes later with the more advanced grips. The slight pushing motion will be accentuated by the toss of the ball. The toss of the ball should be slightly in front of the server. If allowed to drop on the ground, the ball would fall within the area the size of the racket head and in front of, and just to the left of, the left foot. With this grip and this correct toss, the pupil should feel the slight pushing motion. Perhaps another illustration for a correct toss and hit would be helpful: tell your pupil to pretend that he has a wall in front of him, four inches from the baseline. He uses his racket as a hammer, the ball as a nail. If his racket (the hammer) contacts the ball (the nail) fairly flush or head-on, he will be stroking correctly.

Since the toss of the ball is directly related to the stroke itself, I cannot dismiss this fifth element altogether at this point in the lesson. The toss of the ball is with the left arm and hand. After the beginning stance is found, I ask the pupil to place the ball in his left hand against the face of the racket (strings). Then I ask him to place the racket in front of him with the racket completely facing the ball and its intended flight. The arms do not have to be extended. They should be comfortably close to the body. This is important, for it allows a more relaxed feeling before starting the swing.

The swing itself is really quite simple if your pupil is correct in all of his positions up to this point. The swing begins with the racket going down, back, and up to what I call the tray position. During this movement, the player's weight should stay on the back foot (no further backward weight movement is necessary). At this tray position, he will begin his toss of the ball to the correct height, which should be at the point of the full extension of the arm and racket. After the toss, the throwing motion of the racket begins. The weight moves forward as the player's body rotates into the balanced position which marks the conclusion of the swing. The end of the swing should find the racket on the left side of the body and pointing toward the back fence.

The weight transfer in relation to the swing should be a delayed motion. At the moment the ball is tossed, the left heel should return to the ground and the right heel should begin to rise. Try it; it's easy! The weight transfer is made easier through the simple movement of the heels of the feet. The reason for this delayed transfer of weight is that it helps in "tossing the ball to the swing." If the weight is left back too long after the throw, the player will be "swinging to the toss." These are two expressions I often use, and they are entirely different in meaning.

I have found a system of counting that will help you teach the serve. As the swing begins, count "down, back, up, toss, hit, balance." The tempo should be slow and even and can be increased slightly as thought patterns speed up.

One last mention of balance in the swing is necessary—the role of the throwing arm. This arm plays an important part in proper balance for all the tennis strokes. On the serve, the left arm will fall close to the left leg after the toss and remain there until the completion of the swing in an on-balance position. If the serve goes in, the left hand returns to the throat of the racket and adjusts the grip for the forehand stroke.

B. The Volley

(*Welby Van Horn*)

I think of the volley as a stroke. This may seem surprising to you. You may ask—"Isn't it really a block or a punch?" In my opinion, the answer to this question spells the secret to successful volleying for the beginner; it also serves to indicate the direction of the volleyer through our three stages of development.

"Stroke" is a meaningful word to me. We stroke a cat or a dog: stroking, for me, is synonymous with caressing. The word implies feel, delicacy. A tennis racket is similar to many musical instruments. Like a guitar or a violin, it has strings. The better violinists and guitarists "caress" these strings. They have touch—feel. The volley, too, requires caressing the ball to keep it on the racket. Only with this caressing motion will the beginner acquire the feel of the volley.

However, the stroke volley can properly be called a punch or a block volley as a player progresses. Often, the necessity for fast playing action demands this change, a good example of the playing situation shaping the stroke. On the advanced level, as we will note later, the stroke may even become a drive volley on the high shots.

At this point, I would like to add that I do not teach the volley until the student has his balance, grips, and the shape of his groundstrokes reasonably perfected. I start the volley well after the groundstrokes and the serve. The reasons for this are deeply related to my philosophy of developing junior players. First of all, the volley is not a useful weapon for beginning players. We can sum up the uses of the volley for players in this beginning category in three words—*don't use it!* Beginners who find themselves at the net might just as well turn around, run back, and try to catch up to the ball. Second, and even more important, two of the basic ideas I teach on the groundstrokes make the transition to the volley a simple one for the beginner. I use the *same* stroking concept on the groundstrokes; here, too, I want them to "feel" the stroke, to apply a sense of feel through the fingers, and also use the same balance that I teach on the groundstrokes, although there are differences because the follow-through is greatly diminished. The main difference, of course, is that less adjustment of the balance foot is required than on the groundstrokes. On the forehand, however, the right side of the body does not end higher than the left. There is a similarity between backhand volley balance and backhand stroke balance—the left hip should be higher for forward weight distribution.

Stance.

Beginning of Backswing.

Forward Step.

Forward Swing.

Point of Contact.

End of Stroke.

Stance.

Beginning of Backswing.

End of Backswing.

Forward Step.

Forward Swing.

Point of Contact.

End of Stroke.

There are, of course, three differences between the shape of the volley stroke and the shape of the groundstrokes: (1) the stroke is shorter; (2) the path of the racket is *downward*, rather than upward and (3) the racket face is open on both sides (more so on the forehand than the backhand).

The open face and slight downward path of the racket provide a small amount of underspin for control.

For the beginner, the grips are the same as for the groundstrokes. The wrist is firm throughout the stroke.

When the racket is moved up on the backswing, it should go back about as far as the right shoulder on the forehand, the left shoulder on the backhand.

Point of contact is approximately the same as on the groundstrokes—about opposite the left foot on the forehand, just out in front of the right foot on the backhand.

The finish of the stroke is barely beyond the point of contact and barely below it. On the finish, I try to get the racket head slightly *below* the wrist on both forehand and backhand. At the end of the follow-through on the forehand, the butt end of the racket is pointed toward the left hip, not toward the middle of the body. On the backhand, the racket is slightly more parallel to the net. On the backhand, the arm finishes straight; on the forehand, slightly bent.

The step on the volley, as on the groundstrokes, should be in the direction that allows the ball to be hit at a comfortable distance from the body.

By approaching the volley through my definition of "stroke," beginners will be well on the road toward depth, the delicacy of the angle shots, the stop volley, and the lob volley, all of which are important on the level of advanced play.

C. The Lob

It is at the beginning level that our pupils start to develop feel and a knowledge of when to use the lob. Once, recently, I remarked to Welby Van Horn that the lob seems to be a forgotten shot. "It's not!" he replied, "It's a *mad* shot today. They always use it when they are mad!" This is one use of the lob that we won't suggest, of course, but we do start talking about the lob to our pupils as soon as they are able to rally from the baseline. It is, of course, important to them when they begin to play competitively.

A lesson might begin this way: as we are hitting with pupils, we might try them on a very high ball to test their ability to judge descent, to move back toward the fence. They will too frequently hit the ball on too low a trajectory, and so we suggest that whenever we hit the ball high to them, they hit back high to us, even higher, that they "come up" more into the ball and be sure to keep the racket face open. We will explain that their main job under these circumstances will be to move their opponent back for a high ball, and we will indicate the importance of height to give them time to get back into court. And for this very reason, we will suggest the lob when they have been brought outside the sidelines.

One of the most difficult problems for beginners is handling a high backhand. As we have noted, we don't want them to hit one—but often they must. The best way for them to do it is to throw the racket *up over the ball*. They will usually be well back or outside the lines when they make this shot, so the ball should be contacted with an open face. The racket shaft will be almost vertical to the ground as it moves up into the ball, and the tip of the racket goes over the ball in the contact area.

When the playing situation is well back of the baseline, or outside the lines, ball control calls for an open face racket, hitting up, following nearly the same line as the rebounding ball does. It is a defensive shot (it is rather difficult to be in a more defensive position than climbing up a fence), but if the shot is well made—deep enough and high enough—the situation is reversed and the opponent must make this most difficult defensive shot. On this basis, we might call the high defensive lob a very tough attacking shot in beginning tennis.

Eventually, we hope the lob will become a most important shot in our player's repertoire, one that he will be able to make offensively, as well as defensively, once he has developed the touch for it.

Using Underspin on the Forehand Lob.

Using Underspin on the Backhand Lob.

Instead of summing up Part II, we want to add a few points—a potpourri of suggestions, ideas, and methods—and we will begin with a further discussion of the merits of the Big Game in relation to the teaching process.

The Big Game

If the Big Game were the only way to play, then perhaps this is the way we should teach tennis:

There are really only six shots you need on a tennis court. First, there's the most important shot in the game—the serve. We will concentrate on this shot 50 per cent of the time until you have a serve like Kramer's or Gonzales', and this is what you're going to do— you're going to run like mad right after you've made it, and let me show you where you will run to. Here we are, at the net. This is the second most important shot in the game; it's called a volley. You don't let the ball bounce; you hit it in the air. (The game used to be played back there at the baseline, but that's the old-fashioned way. They let the ball bounce; *then* they hit it. They called it a ground-stroke. Don't let me catch you doing that—except *once*, and I'll tell you about that in a minute.)

Now, take a look out there, from here at the net. Notice how much of the court you can see, how much of the court you can hit into. If you were back behind that baseline rallying, you would not be able to see the whole court, would you? And so you'd just have to hit them deep. Up here you can put the ball away very quickly. Now, move back a bit, because you won't always be able to hit the ball this close to the net; you'll have to volley from farther back, and sometimes you'll hit the ball after it bounces. But that's all right; that's a half-volley, and a half-volley is not a groundstroke. It's a half-volley, and I want you to be able to do that because you will be doing it on the baseline, too.

Every now and then, someone is going to try to hit the ball over your head, so you're going to hit a serve, running in or running back—it's called an overhead.

Now let me show you the fifth shot. It's called return of serve.

9 | ADDING A FEW POINTS

It's too bad, but you're going to have to let the ball bounce on this one; the rules say so. Since you do have to let it bounce, we're not going to work on this return of serve for quite a while, because it isn't too important. Really, all you have to do is hit the ball hard enough to put it by your opponent or through him.

And now for the last shot. Occasionally, you're going to be playing against those old-fashioned players who hit the ball from the baseline. There are one or two of them still around, and they do a very stupid thing: they hit the ball short every now and then, and just in case you forget what I'm teaching you and get caught on that baseline once, you might have to hit a short ball. But we won't call it a groundstroke; it's really an approach shot.

There you are. That's all we're going to be working on—*the serve, the volley, the half-volley, the overhead, the return of serve,* and *the approach shot.*

H'm'm. Sounds like our next national champion, doesn't it? But actually, the passage above is about three hundred words of sheer heresy to most of us in tennis teaching. We plod along on somewhat diverse routes toward the same goal—the development of sound groundstrokes. Why? It might be because some of us believe that the great returns of serve, the passing shots, and yes, even the great approach shots, all emerge from *a sound background in the groundstrokes.* It might be that we want to keep pupils out of situations they can't handle. Or it might be because a particular pupil is not destined to play the Big Game ever. Probably, we concentrate on groundstrokes for all these reasons.

We may start, as Bill Murphy does, by letting pupils hit a few balls before we have told them anything at all. This is an excellent approach because it shows us what we need to concentrate on from the very start. It may be a sloppy wrist action, a tendency to hit down on the ball, imbalance, tension, or hard hitting—whatever it is, it's helpful to know what each beginner will do without any preconceived ideas about what he should do. We might give them a lesson or two on balance—even without a racket, or start them a few feet from the net, just popping the ball into court. We might, of course, combine all three techniques in one lesson, and even add a word or two about the hitting area.

And so we plod along—making "X's" and putting "six balls in a row on the court" and "pressing" wrists and "choking up" grips and telling them "not to let a two-ounce ball put them off balance" and asking them to "finish their stroke," to keep the racket going until the ball bounces on the other side, to "count one thousand one, one thousand two, one thousand three," to "pose."

We work *always*, through any of these methods, to teach them to control themselves and their rackets. We might say, as Van Horn does, "Imagine that you're in a narrow alleyway, with walls on each side; swing your forehand without hitting the wall on your left, and your backhand without hitting the wall on your right."

We use every prop or gimmick we can get our hands on—ball machines, stroke groovers, and tether balls or backboards (always advising them to start well back from the backboard so that they have time to complete each stroke).

Van Horn finds the tether ball his most useful teaching aid and uses it this way:

Tennis Practice-Set

The pupil hits the ball high and allows it to bounce twice, always hitting on the descent, of course, and practicing one stroke at a time. This is good exercise in waiting for the ball. Then the pupil can alternate forehands and backhands. This speeds up the acquisition of grip change and body-turn. It can next be used to teach facility in moving up and back by hitting on one bounce, then on two, one stroke at a time as a first step. Then two bounces for the forehand, one on the backhand and then the opposite. As an exercise to assure an early backswing, when the pupil is ready he can use it up close to the first bounce.

We teach in progressive steps, often "feeding" pupils balls on the same side of the net, and when we have gained some control on the forehand and backhand, we spend some time having pupils alternate shots to get used to grips. And finally, we work back to the baseline, spending some time on such a simple thing as helping them start a rally.

Starting a Rally

Where to drop the ball is the important thing for pupils to know in starting a rally. On the forehand they must drop it well out in front of the left foot, for this reason: they should take a short step toward the net with their left foot just before the swing. If the ball is dropped by the foot, the racket will contact the ball at about the belt buckle, too far back to be in our range of correctness. This may seem to be a small point, but it is an important one. Dropping the ball too far back can keep the pupil from getting off the ground on the very first crack of the ball, and the drop should be a gentle one, with just enough impetus to bring the ball back up to the waist. It is important, too, at the start, to have pupils hold the racket back in hitting position, ready to hit the ball when they drop it. Otherwise, they will have to swing back and forward too fast to control the racket.

Starting a rally is really difficult for beginners. Often the only fun they may have at this point is getting off one good hit from their hand every now and then, and it's not a bad idea to have them make a game of it. It is no small accomplishment for some of them!

Of course, their task is more than merely hitting the ball into court: they must be *placing it*, to make it easy for their fellow rallyer to attempt a return. Here you should stress a slow, easy swing. A ball that is hit well up over the net and straight at the person on the other side is what you want.

There is a final point connected with rallying: beginners should start these rallies about three to six feet behind the baseline. Often you see neophytes starting on or inside the baseline, then wandering around in this area, only to dash madly back when the ball is hit deep. Tell pupils not to worry about the short ones. Let them hit balls on the fifth bounce for now, if necessary, rather than rushing up and losing their swings. *They must learn early to respect "No-Man's-Land."*

While we lead them up to rallying, we are working on the serve, of course. Some of us might start in the very first lesson. The sooner they can play, the more fun they will have. But keep this point in mind—*overencouraging competition* can be a mistake. If pupils think the only goal at this time is winning, all the work we are doing can go for naught. It is far more important for them to concentrate on the principles of sound ball control.

At the right time, we will start them on the volley. There is considerable difference of opinion as to the right time; but because, as we stated earlier, it takes the average pupil more time to become at home at the net than at the baseline, it should never be postponed too long.

Certainly there are differences—a diversity of routes—in teaching. It would not suit any of us to teach exactly as another teaches. Take the serve, for instance. In my opinion, Van Horn's view of the serve—as a skill developed over a long time, depending on what the pupils can do in the various stages of development—is a sound one. Few beginners can understand and perform the correct wrist or hand action with the correct service grip, and this is the crux of the serve. The Van Horn method is a painstaking, meticulous way to develop the serve, and one I can recommend most highly, but not every teacher will follow this exact pattern. For instance, here is the Van der Meer approach:

The Serve

I start the lesson by demonstrating an orthodox flat serve as used by an experienced player and then tell the pupil that he will be able to acquire a facsimile of what he has just seen, in a few minutes, provided he follows my step-by-step sequence.

I explain the stance to him by drawing an arrow on the ground at the baseline in the exact direction the pupil will send the ball. The pupil has to cover the left-hand point of the arrow with his left foot. The right foot is put at right angles with the arrow shaft, the width of the shoulders. The head of the racket is held, raised in line with the arrow, at shoulder-height. Once this principle of the stance has been understood, the pupil will never have difficulty again in serving to the different service squares. The grip is the same as the forehand grip used by the pupil.

The pupil is asked to "reach" with his left hand towards the sky as far as possible, and just to repeat the movement a few times. The second step is to toss the ball slightly higher than the pupil would be able to reach with his racket, and to catch the ball in his outstretched hand. I explain that this is very important because this is a measurable clue for the pupil to see how accurate his toss-up is. As soon as he can catch the ball in his outstretched hand without moving the hand, we are ready for the next step. I now ask him to extend his racket arm to its full length; to hold it here, toss the ball up and just gently touch the ball with the racket-face.

The next step is to give the ball a slight tap with a three to four inch motion of the racket; then the elbow is gradually bent and the tap motion followed until the hand touches the back of the pupil's head. The next step from here is to ask the pupil not to stop at the tap, but to swing right through after the point of contact.

Next, we must put the left arm and the racket arm together!

I ask my pupil to swing the racket down from the starting point and back, until his hand touches his head (or if it is easier for him to understand—until his racket touches his back), and at the same time to extend his left arm toward the sky. As soon as this synchronized movement can be done fluently, I ask the pupil to repeat the movement just as before, but to release and catch the ball. If this can be done, I turn my pupil around to face the fence, and then I have him go through the motions he has learned, this time reaching up and swinging at the ball. (I use the fence so that the pupil will not have to worry about getting the ball over the net and into court.) After a few successful contacts, I let him serve from the service-line across the net, and then move him to the baseline. He can now produce a full facsimile of a complete serve.

All this should take from fifteen to twenty minutes. Once the pupil has had this initial success, I start breaking the stroke down again and work on each area separately.

To show further diversity in approaches, we should make room for the teaching of the block volley at the start.

The Block Volley

Many instructors prefer to start a pupil with the block volley. This approach is particularly applicable to pupils of less natural ability and pupils who cannot control overswinging at the ball.

It is the direct opposite of the stroke approach. The name "block volley" describes the technique most adequately. The pupil merely blocks the ball well out in front of him. There is no backswing at all; rather, there is an immediate reaching out in front, on both backhand and forehand sides.

The backhand grip is the same as that used for the backhand drive, a full Eastern grip. The regular forehand grip can be used, or a slight move toward the Western to bring the hand behind the racket face. This necessitates a somewhat broad change of grips, but this is no problem in beginning or intermediate tennis, and can only become one in advanced tennis on the championship level. This approach sets an early point of contact in the very beginning, a somewhat earlier point of contact, in fact, than on the stroke volley.

There is no wrist action on this volley. Speed is obtained through the forearm and the weight transfer. The racket stops approximately *on contact* with the ball.

So, we've added quite a few points. None of this diversity should be considered confusing, however; it's all part of the fun of the game. The teaching of tennis is a trial-and-error process (Chet Murphy has a better definition for it—"progressive approximation"), in which the pupil is led, through a labyrinth of cues and corrective techniques (and quite possibly, varying approaches), to ball control, the right way for *him* to control the ball. The same is true of a teacher. For him, also, it is a process of "progressive approximation," trying a new concept here, a new method there, until he pulls out of the tremendous grab bag of ideas his own way to teach the game. We can sincerely hope that in teaching the beginner he not in any way approximate our little satire on teaching the Big Game. Later, on the advanced level of play, we would not quarrel with him (for he may have the next national champion on his hands), but for now he had better grub along with the rest of us, never forgetting that the sum of what he is teaching— self-discipline, the fun and sense of accomplishment in working at something and doing it right—is a bit bigger than the game itself.

The Intermediate

The road ahead is more difficult for both teacher and pupil. There was considerable sameness to teaching beginners. There was little we could tell the beginner about strategy and tactics, because there was little that he could do, and all his opponents played about the same way, with the same weaknesses. In shaping his strokes, individualization was at a minimum; possibly we attempted to fit all beginners to our favorite look. There was no variety in stroke equipment, either; no need to concern ourselves with underspin or topspin on the groundstrokes; no concern for spin on the serve. We introduced the volley and had him practice it, but warned him that he would not find it a useful weapon at that stage.

Beginners are all "rallyers," developing sound flat drives and sound service action that produces consistent flat serves; strategically, they are steady pushers. But in the intermediate stage, individual differences must be taken into account in the shaping of the strokes, and the playing situations will make variety in the shape of the strokes a necessity.

In fact, because of psychological or physical problems, it may prove difficult to move any one of the strokes through the intermediate level. There are times when it takes special know-how plus imagination to keep the basic drives on the right track. This problem is compounded by the fact that we will want to introduce underspin somewhere along the way.

This may seem a grim picture, but actually we find a pleasant metamorphosis taking place. As an intermediate, your pupil is beginning to *look* like a tennis player. He is developing concentration. His reactions are improving. There's a bounce in his step and balance in his footwork. His wrist is firming up. He is finding his timing. He is hitting harder, and his balls have less height over the net. He is beginning to develop the control that will enable you to lead him through all the possibilities in the game. He may even be developing a groundstroke strength on his forehand side.

THE ROAD AHEAD 10

Certainly all the strategical and tactical essentials that we developed in the beginner (steadiness, depth, and playing to a backhand) remain an integral part of the intermediate's game. One of the keys to his success will be the continual development of these abilities.

Van Horn calls tennis a game in which the offense is played into a backhand, and so we continue to stress this, anticipating the advanced level. Chet Murphy expresses one of the goals for our intermediate this way:

> The intermediate must be able to match his opponent "backhand for backhand," to spar with him on his backhand, so that he gets the first chance to score a knockout with his forehand.
>
> In a sense, tennis is like boxing; we see numerous little harmless sparring blows for every knockout blow. Boxers spar with each other until an opening occurs, or is created by fakes, feints, moves, quickness, a sudden change in tempo. And so it should be in tennis—you should spar with him, but spar on his weak stroke (the backhand, usually, for intermediates as well as beginners). However, he, too, may be a smart tennis player, and will want to spar with you. In that case, you have to be able to match him deep backhand for deep backhand, until he gives you the first chance to do something else—to start knocking him out by running him past his right sideline with your forehand, or merely moving him over so that you can play his backhand again, or by pushing him back as you approach the net, or by fooling him with a drop shot, or luring him up with a short ball to his backhand. In any case, you must first be able to spar with him—backhand to backhand—deep to his backhand, so that you get the first chance to determine how the sparring is to end.

It will be some time before our intermediate will have the ball control to perform all this, of course, and he will be doing so always within our basic framework of position tennis.

To outline the goals ahead for the intermediate, in terms of strokes: (1) he will concentrate more and more on his volley; (2) he will groove his basic drives; (3) he will develop one or more kinds of spin on his serve; (4) he will concentrate on learning to use underspin and topspin; (5) he will "forget" his strokes as he goes along. Strategically and tactically he will: (1) take the ball earlier, (2) learn position tennis, (3) learn to play a greater variety of weaknesses, (4) make the transition from defense to offense, (5) use his strength, (if he has one), and (6) use more of his opponent's court.

A. Ball Control

"Flat" was the key word for the beginners' strokes—forehand, backhand, and serve. But spin now becomes more and more important—topspin, underspin, even sidespin on the groundstrokes for the intermediate, and either sidespin (slice) or overspin, possibly both, on the serve.

A competent teacher will now need to know considerably more about spin and the methods to obtain it. Conceivably, with basic drives, he *could* stick to the basic concept of control as outlined for a beginner: the racket swinging up through the ball sets a level of flight and automatically places topspin on the ball; on the forehand, the racket face is flat, "on edge," throughout the whole swing; on the backhand, the racket face is open at the end of the backswing, flat throughout the hitting area, and flat at the end of the swing. The only difference he would suggest, to get topspin, would be a slightly more upward swing. However, presenting any concept of control as the only way to hit a ball would belie two of the basic premises of this book—that tennis games are tailor-made to individual differences and that there are a variety of ways to control the ball and to play it.

There are many ways to add topspin besides coming up to the ball more. If we contact the ball with a slightly closed racket face, we will apply topspin. This certainly requires a more upward swing to offset the angle of the racket, and it also requires more speed of swing. Many good forehands have been hit in this manner, but it is not recommended for the backhand. In this method, the ball is covered at contact, as the top edge of the racket is ahead of the bottom edge. However, meeting the ball with a flat racket and covering it during the contact area is a more acceptable technique on the forehand side. Primarily, this is done through a rotation of the forearm and a slight elbow bend. To repeat: the hand should

THE STRATEGICAL FRAMEWORK 11

Using Underspin on the Forehand.

Using Underspin on the Backhand.

not be turned over the ball consciously. We have already mentioned the rotating forearm in Part II. This rotation is a legitimate way to obtain topspin or, as we indicated, to get general control of the ball on the forehand side, if it is a pupil's natural tendency. In fact, both speed and control may be added through a strong forearm action just before contact. Van Horn teaches topspin by suggesting "a slightly rising right side." Chet Murphy suggests raising the right elbow on cross-court passing shots. These techniques apply to the forehand only.

The intermediate has no business attempting to "cover" his backhand. Topspin should be obtained only by a more upward swing, with the racket contacting the ball either open or flat.

Underspin has come a long way—from "unfair tactics" to "mechanically unsound" to the "only way to hit a backhand," as we hear it called in some quarters. It is considered more important on the backhand side by almost everyone, but it can certainly be a most useful addition to the forehand as well.

Van Horn summarizes the use of spin for the three levels this way:

> The beginner should be cautioned against attempting underspin. Even topspin, far more important to the intermediate than underspin, should be eliminated from the beginner's choice of strokes. The ability to execute all the spin strokes is the eventual, but not the immediate, goal. An advanced player should have a complete repertoire of underspin strokes and should know the occasions on which they can best be put to use.

If we think of the Van Horn stroke volley, the backhand slice can be called an elongated volley. To achieve underspin, it is only necessary to add a longer backswing and a longer follow-through. But there are, of course, variations in underspin. There is the "chip," for instance. It is made with a short backswing and, usually, a more downward motion. And finally, there is sidespin, in which the racket contacts the ball on the inside of the hitter's body.

All of these spins are used for only one purpose—ball control—and they are related always to the tactical situation.

B. Ball Control and Intermediate Tactics

Increasingly it will become evident that ball control and tactics are intertwined, that the playing situation determines the shape of the stroke, as full-size strokes become short ones, and varying degrees of topspin and underspin are added in the intermediate progression. Flexibility, rather than a sameness of stroke production, becomes the key as a player progresses. When the pupil is hitting harder, the force of gravity is less of an ally and topspin becomes more important.

We can always view our player in terms of his opponent, keeping in mind that from time to time he will now be playing players who are in a more mature stage of development. This situation becomes one of the most important factors in his improvement from now on. From the general suggestions we make to him, the talented pupil will often almost automatically adapt to varying playing situations and what Bill Lufler calls "the increasing variety in the rhythm of the game." No matter how many times we plead for sounder defense, quicker reactions, and more concentration, an intermediate often learns the lesson best as he battles a much better player and realizes that he *must* get a lot of balls back into court if he is to beat a good player, that he *must* react faster and faster, and that he *must* concentrate all the way through a match.

Therefore, our player takes the ball earlier on the bounce, not just because he is gaining the control to do so, but because he will be out of position if he does not. His opponent will be able to hit drop shots and short balls, but the intermediate plays closer to the baseline, also, because in a later stage he will want to take advantage of short balls that are his opponent's mistakes. And this points up the first use of underspin—the backhand slice on high balls.

We will, of course, have him take return of serve earlier because the tempo has increased, and because he will be hitting higher balls on serve returns, he will learn to block or chip the ball on both sides. Short swings and underspin are important, too, on first fast serves.

Basically, what we are doing in the intermediate stage is continually strengthening the player's defense. Using the short block return of serve is an example of this, and when his opponent moves him wide of the court, we will suggest that he use underspin on both sides again, with a short swing.

At the end of the intermediate stage, our player makes his first transition from defense to attack. He comes in behind the short ball. On the backhand, underspin is recommended on all approach shots, whether the ball is above or below the net. The forehand can be made flat or with some topspin on balls above the net, but underspin should also be used when the ball is low. On both backhand and forehand, the swings will be short because of the playing situations. A small amount of sidespin may develop here on the down-the-line shots.

Because our player is taking the ball earlier, he will be able to use more of the court. At the end of the intermediate stage we will be talking about more than merely deep cross-court hitting from the baseline. Primarily, this change is preparation for the advanced level.

The player must keep in mind at all times that there is a difference between what he is practicing and *what he can use* in competitive play. There is, too,

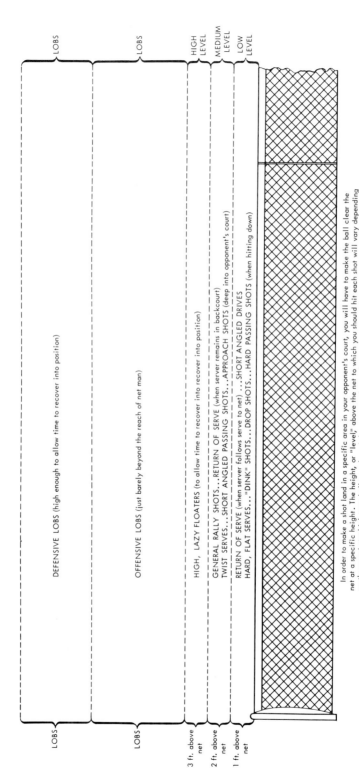

LOBS

DEFENSIVE LOBS (high enough to allow time to recover into position)

LOBS

OFFENSIVE LOBS (just barely beyond the reach of net man)

HIGH LEVEL

HIGH, LAZY FLOATERS (to allow time to recover into position)

GENERAL RALLY SHOTS...RETURN OF SERVE (when server remains in backcourt)
TWIST SERVES...SHORT ANGLED PASSING SHOTS...APPROACH SHOTS (deep into opponent's court)

MEDIUM LEVEL

RETURN OF SERVE (when server follows serve to net) ...SHORT ANGLED DRIVES
HARD, FLAT SERVES..."DINK" SHOTS...DROP SHOTS...HARD PASSING SHOTS (when hitting down)

LOW LEVEL

3 ft. above net

2 ft. above net

1 ft. above net

In order to make a shot land in a specific area in your opponent's court, you will have to make the ball clear the net at a specific height. The height, or "level" above the net to which you should hit each shot will vary depending on the speed at which your ball travels and the purpose of your shot, and your position.

Passing shots, for example, meant to cause the net man to hit at a low volley, should be hit to the low level. Some other shots, intended for more depth, should be hit to a higher level. General rally shots should clear the net by about two or three feet.

If your shots are landing short, and you want more depth, it may be necessary to hit higher as well as harder. Learn to "hit into "levels."

a time element involved—a long pause after each stage, while the practicing is going on—before a player will be able to use successfully the new material he has been given.

Because we want to introduce the idea of using more of an opponent's court and because our player's defensive game must be strengthened in terms of his opponent's transition from defense to attack, controlling the depth of his shots in terms of shortness as well as length, becomes important. This involves what Chet Murphy calls "hitting into levels."

One important factor in depth control comes from controlling the height at which the ball clears the net as well as from controlling the speed at which the ball travels. At times, in order to get more depth, a player must hit higher as well as harder. One must select a different height above the net for each shot, and the height will vary, depending on the speed at which the ball is struck and the purpose of the shot. Therefore, one should aim first to hit the ball into a "level" above the net, and aim secondly to hit the ball into a certain portion or spot in the opponent's court.

We have a chart that illustrates this concept of "hitting into levels." It indicates also the "levels" to be selected for various specific shots. Notice on the chart that "general rally shots" are placed on the medium "level," i.e., about two feet above the net. If they are hit into this "level" with only a medium amount of speed, these shots are likely to land deep in the opponent's court, causing him to hit from behind his baseline. The opponent will thus be made either to remain in the backcourt, or if he insists upon going to the net, to make a hazardous approach. If this height of two feet above the net seems surprising, let me remind the reader that Kramer has stated that most of his rally shots clear the net by about two feet and some by as much as three feet.

The diagram also indicates the different "levels" into which a baseliner should aim his groundstrokes, once his opponent has advanced to the forecourt. By hitting at a medium speed and merely changing the height or "level" by which the ball clears the net, the baseliner can cause the net man to hit at low volleys or half-volleys.

"Hitting into levels" is important to the intermediate as we require him to modify the height of his shots in relation to new tactics. This is particularly true in his last stage of development, when he defends against a net attack, and when he needs to do some minor maneuvering to win.

This concept, along with all the other ideas suggested in this chapter, points out how on the intermediate level we are always teaching ball control with the winning tactics in mind. On the beginning level, ball control was the dominant factor; now for the intermediate, the two emphases become inseparable except for the occasional isolated grooving of the strokes.

C. The Philosophy of Defense

(Welby Van Horn)

The major theme throughout this book is that winning tennis under any conditions, at all levels of play, is dependent on the player's ability to defend.

This was the winning formula of great players in the past; it is the winning formula of the great players today, and it will not change in the future.

This formula requires a mastery of sound forehand and backhand ground-strokes which enable a player to maintain depth, to develop a consistent return of serve and the important passing shots. And it means, too, mastery over that most neglected shot in tennis today—the lob. This defensive ability was, and still is, the equipment of the great players. Tilden, Perry, Vines, Budge, and Kramer were attackers, yes. Their serves were potent weapons; their volleys and overheads were devastating, *but they were defensive giants as well.* They could defend all areas of their court from attack because they could use their opponents' whole court. At times of attack, touch, dexterity, and consistency were no strangers to them. Gonzales and Rosewall were defenders also. Rosewall, of course, is a prime example of the importance of defense. A small man with an average serve, at his peak he ranked above all the other players in the world.

It is important, then, that all teachers implant this basic philosophy of the game in every pupil. However, the net-rushing tactics prevalent in the game today make teaching defense a most difficult and frustrating task.

Every instructor knows the exciting experience of teaching a young student who has, at first appearance, all the potential of a fine player. Emotional stability, desire, concentration, physical coordination, intelligence—these are the essentials that promise the possibility of rapid improvement. Such characteristics make the initial teaching job a pleasant one. The period during which the strokes begin to take shape (sometimes a long and painful one for the less gifted student) is shortened. The coach's reservoir of patience is barely tapped, and his teaching vocabulary is not strained.

The real challenge to this teaching ability appears, however, when the the able student's strokes progress to the point at which he can concentrate more on game patterns than on stroke patterns. For if a young player is to fulfill his potential, he must be taught to see the game as a whole; he must become familiar with the basic tactical necessities of winning tennis practiced by all the champions, past and present. He must learn that defensive patterns are just as important to successful tennis as offensive patterns. To communicate this knowledge to the young player and to convince him of its importance is one of the most formidable problems that confront the instructor. Young tennis players are often idolaters who seek to mimic the champion and, as a result, attempt too soon to copy the Big Game tactics of serving and rushing the net. When they do this, ignoring the advice of their instructors, it is not too much to say that they become the instruments of their own destruction. They become emotional victims of the Big Game they seek to emulate, and if they persist in this narrow-minded pattern of play they will eventually encounter the gigantic frustration of inconsistency, an encounter which can lead only to a complete loss of confidence in themselves and in their game. When this happens, "all the King's men"—much less an instructor—would find it difficult to put the pieces together again.

To the young and aspiring player, the occasions for useful and effective defense in men's championship tennis seem trivial when compared to the gloriously destructive power of the serve, volley, and overhead smash. How does one explain convincingly that the ability to execute excellent defensive counterstrokes (the timely lob, the unspectacular consistency of service return, the controlled depth of forehand and backhand groundstrokes) is the difference between the great and the near-great—the difference between winning or losing the big matches?

This, then, is a major problem facing all instructors—to explain successfully the pitfalls of practicing the Big Game too soon. The novice, intermediate, and junior players with promise can see only the *end result* embodied in the champion; and rarely do they attach any importance to the effectiveness of defense as used by the champion. Big Game tactics tend to warp the minds of *most* players at all levels, making them assume that the primary objective is to win the point quickly; they assume that the percentage is against the player who returns the ball too often. Even on today's championship level very few players supplement their Big Game tactics with sound defense. The top players do, of course, and this is why they are superior.

Perhaps there is another factor which tends to shape our thoughts with regard to winning in any sport. While tennis tactics have changed considerably since 1948 and the emergence of Jack Kramer as an exponent of the Big Game at its best, other sports have also shed the cloak of caution for that of aggression. Basketball, football, and baseball scores have soared to unprecedented heights. Even so, the real students of all sports realize that few coaches worth anything would neglect the first fundamental—defense. The old axioms, "A good defense is the best offense," and "If they can't score on you, they can't beat you," are fighting for survival under the spectators' desire for more action, more scoring. However, I believe these axioms will continue to survive and are as practical today as ever. Naturally, the ultimate goal is to achieve a delicate balance that will allow one to administer the *coup de grace* of offensive play while executing a clever counter to the offensive game.

In tennis you must first establish a sound, orthodox attitude toward improvement. This calls for proper balance as applied through footwork; it places a premium on proper grip; it demands a shaping of the correct swing patterns in forehand and backhand groundstrokes, in the serve, and in the volley and overhead smash. It also necessitates an unswerving dedication of the student in resisting the temptation of the Big Game at an early stage of development. Above all, to recognize this necessity demands the intelligence and faith of the student as well as the conviction and constant reminders of the instructor.

A. Shaping the Strokes

THE GROUNDSTROKES

Now we are concerned with a most pleasant process that might be called "putting the final touches on the groundstrokes." As the broad outlines of the strokes take shape, the details become more important.

This stage is rather exciting, for we are watching the emergence of a tennis player! The first sign we see is that the groundstrokes are well on the way. We can sit back now, with a sigh of relief, and say, "Good! Fine! We'll work on strokes from time to time, but now let's bring the serve and the volley into the limelight a bit."

Remember, however, we are concerned with individual differences. There is only one solution to the problem of handling individual differences—experience. What is required of you to help your pupil is experience plus your knowledge of all the mechanics and dynamics that we have discussed thus far and their application to each individual problem. Nevertheless, some general discussion of a few ideas may prove helpful.

Despite the fact that our intermediate at this stage, and often well beyond it, is still working from time to time on the groundstrokes, two points become more and more important: (1) It is not possible to hit a tennis ball well when you are thinking about *how* to hit it, and (2) the strokes must build on themselves.

From now on, as our pupil increases the amount of his competitive play, he must be able to "forget" his strokes during matches, though he can think about them in practice and continue to work on them in lessons. His goal, which he is fast reaching, is to concentrate on thinking about *where* to hit. He is also reaching the point at which competition will

12 THE TRANSITIONAL STAGE

build his strokes, rather than hinder them. It is important for this process to take place, and if the strokes are *not* building on themselves, the work of both pupil and instructor is greatly increased.

Often it is out of his play that we can sense the direction in which a player is going—the many minor differences in backswing, forward swing, and ending. Of course, we want to see that ball cushioned in the racket on both sides. We want to see the early unhurried backswing, and the fairly flat ending, but by no means all players will obtain the same length in the contact area. Not all players will be attuned to the slow sweeping deliberate strokes that most of us like to see, and some will find it far more natural to cover the ball on the forehand, to hit with an open face or flat face, even to use underspin on the backhand.

These are some of the individual differences that appear now and that we must consider as we attempt to groove the strokes.

So what if they can't all obtain the same length in the contact area? It is very easy for us to overstress the hitting area and end up with an over-straight arm that has eliminated the relaxation period after contact. It is perfectly possible to say that in a well-hit forehand or backhand drive, there is a feeling of "going around the ball," which would mean less of a pressed look on the forehand and less of a straight-arm ending. It is easy for us to go too far out on a limb with any of the theories of dynamics and mechanics. Somewhere between yesterday's fancier forehands with the high backswings, the extreme covering of the ball, the wrapped-around-the-neck ending, and today's tendency toward the straight flat ending, there can be a happy medium if individual differences require it.

Many of us consider the backhand a far easier stroke to set than the forehand because it is somewhat easier for a player to go out on the ball on the backhand side. Most often, however, backhand development will take longer than the forehand development, so let's discuss for a while the development of the backhand in terms of individual differences. Basically, we can break the backhand down into three different types—flat (with the possibility of a slight covering of the ball), open face, and slice. The Addie backhand, for the purpose of definition, I am going to refer to as the Budge-Stow backhand. (There are some minor differences; for instance, the Budge-Stow backhand has a circular backswing.) Tom Stow is the former Berkeley Tennis Club professional who worked with Don Budge and has set a definite style in the teaching of the backhand. One of its main characteristics is a flat racket face at point of contact, throughout contact and at the ending. It can be spoken of as a "lift" and is a topspin shot to one degree or another, depending on the amount of lift. Often teachers gain reputations for teaching one stroke or another; certainly Tom Stow is known for his teaching of the backhand. It was easy to pick out Stow pupils, when he was teaching, by their sound backhands.

The Budge backhand was far more than this basic flat backhand; Budge, using this basic style, could do anything from the backhand side. Unquestionably, many would consider it the most flexible backhand the game has ever seen. It was all the backhands wrapped into one—the ease of swing, the way the whole body flowed into the shot, the power he obtained through proper rotation—it was a thing of beauty and poetry in motion.

To teach all the subtlety, the nuances that Budge was capable of, would be impossible; but the basic flat-faced Budge-Stow topspin backhand can be taught, as Pauline Betz Addie has indicated. It may, however, have gone somewhat out of style in favor of the open-faced backhand, which is exemplified in the pictures of Welby Van Horn. It is certainly more prevalent today.

There is another theory connected with hitting the backhand—that it is best controlled with underspin. The Rosewall backhand, one of the great ones of all time, is a good example.

Now, how does all this affect our teaching at this point? Precisely this way: if a pupil is gaining more control with a particular technique at this time, including the use of underspin, let's let him use it.

A player will evolve naturally into more of a topspin player or more of an underspin player for many reasons. Our concern here is the same as it was for the beginner—ball control—and none of our basic premises have changed. Individual differences have merely compounded the tasks somewhat. What we are interested in now is results in our pupil's playing. The pragmatic attitude is, "What works, counts." Once we have encouraged our player to use underspin on the high backhand, if he becomes a bit enamored of underspin and tends to use it more frequently on the backhand as he progresses, so what? Our "pusher from California" uses it, and Fred Perry and Vines and Kramer and Budge and Bobby Riggs—and that is enough, because (to take just one of these) many of us feel that what was good enough for Court-General Riggs is good enough for a whole country of players.

The gist of this discourse on spin is this—we are not going to sit on the sideline and say, "H'mm, look at that topspin," or "see that underspin"; we are going to say, "Aha, that's one more ball back, and one more, and still another!"

However, if our introduction of underspin has the opposite effect—a loss of control—we had better bring the pupil back immediately to our basic concept of control, keeping in mind that what we are looking for in this stage of development is his one best way to control the ball.

THE SERVE

(*Welby Van Horn*)

The intermediate must now make some of the key changes that will begin to mold his serve and bring it closer to the look of the advanced player.

He should, first of all, make a slight change from the Western grip or modified Western grip that he used as a beginner, to the Eastern forehand grip. The stance remains the same.

Since he will be using the Eastern forehand grip, the face of the racket during the first half of the backswing will be slightly more perpendicular to the court surface than it was with the Western grip. The racket will go back closer to the typical "scratch the back" position of the advanced serve, thus necessitating more of a "loop" than the beginner's serve did.

The intermediate will begin to synchronize his toss with his swing. The toss will be made sooner. In addition, the toss will be made back farther because of the change of grip. Now, if the ball were allowed to drop, it would hit the left foot.

At the start of the serve, the balance is the same as the beginner's balance. However, there is more left turn of the right hip as the ball is tossed. Also, the forward weight distribution begins sooner. The right foot should stay back most of the time; *always* in practice. However, at a later stage of development, because he is beginning to think of advanced tactics (one of which would be to rush the net behind his serve), the intermediate can bring the right foot over occasionally.

As a result of the change of grip, the difference in toss, and the weight distribution, the service takes on a feeling of pulling. This pulling motion creates a more severe lowering of the left shoulder as the ball is hit.

On this intermediate level, we teach slice or overspin. Pupils should use the one with which they get the best results. Because the serve is now more of a pull than a push, and because there is more control, the pupil can concentrate more on hitting to weaknesses.

THE VOLLEY AND THE HALF-VOLLEY

An important task for us in working with our intermediate is to bring his volley up to the quality of his groundstrokes. Up to this point we have been making the volley as easy for him as possible, by having him stand close to the net. Now he should stand back farther to practice low volleys and half-volleys.

Keep in mind that the volley has different sizes, just as the groundstrokes have. Whether you have taught the volley from the Van Horn point of view or started your pupil with the block volley, he must learn that fast balls need no more than a simple blocking motion and slower balls require more swing to obtain pace.

One of the most common flaws we find in our pupil's volley is the tendency to overswing at the ball, very often with easy-looking set-ups and high balls. Too frequently the beginning volleyer will want to kill this ball with what amounts to almost a full stroke. This is *advanced*, not intermediate, tennis: more specifically, the province of a championship class advanced player.

Stance. Note change of grip.

Beginning of Backswing.

The Toss.

Shaping the Loop. In the inter-mediate serve we begin to shape the loop. Note that racket comes into the ball at a slight angle and the face is beveled to put side spin on the ball.

Point of Contact. This is slightly farther back in the intermediate than in the beginner's serve.

End of Stroke. Note that the right foot remains back, but has adjusted as in the forehand to facilitate balance and rotation.

The volley is a "touch" and "finesse" stroke. Nowhere in tennis is *balance* more important. Look at the pictures of volleyers. Note the balancing effect of the left arm; even the hand is poised to indicate the delicacy of the shot.

Once the mechanics of the volley are acquired, only much practice and play will further develop the volleyer. These are the steps, and they are some distance apart: first, the acquiring of the mechanics, then the ability to use the volley well as a practice shot, and finally, the reactions, position, and common-sense placement that bring off the successful volley in actual competition.

All intermediates should be encouraged to spend considerable time just inside or behind the service line practicing the volley and the half-volley. (Underspin and overspin are both applicable to the half-volley.)

B. Reactions and Moving

Now the view from your pupil's court has changed: the tempo has been stepped up; the balls have less loft; his opponents are no longer playing from six feet behind the baseline to the fence (nor is your pupil); his opponents may have developed a strength (probably a forehand) that means placements on any surface if your pupil's court position is not maintained. His opponents may also be able to run him wide of the court. All of this will demand some changes in your pupil's game: concentration must be keener, reactions sharper, footwork faster. More and more, the ball leaving an opponent's racket is like the starting gun on a track field. Early preparation is even more important now, and often the intermediate is so busy getting to the ball that he doesn't prepare for the shot.

Footwork must be accelerated; even if the ball is not far away, it is more difficult to handle because of its increased speed. Whereas once we worked on our pupil's "holding his endings," now we are more concerned with the return, more conscious of his getting back into position.

In short, your player must now become a hustler, a scrambler. Three of the keys to better tennis now are (1) increased concentration, (2) quicker reaction, and (3) ability to move.

Your pupil must learn to shut out everything but himself, the ball, and his opponent. The ability to concentrate will be one of the most important factors in his improvement; however, concentration is not enough. There must be a heightening of reactions, recognition of the fact that the ball must be reacted to the instant it leaves an opponent's racket.

Here is a tip from Chet Murphy about reactions and concentration:

In military service training in aircraft recognition courses, we were taught to see and to recognize aircraft shapes and silhouettes when they were flashed on a screen for 1/100th of a second. We learned to do this, and even to count how many planes we saw in that short period of time.

When training began, we were told that we had all formed the habit of *seeing things at a convenient rate*, and that we could learn, through training, to see them at a much faster rate. After three months of training, we were able to see and recognize things when flashed on the screen for 1/50th or 1/100th of a second.

I believe the same is often true of tennis players. We have all formed the habit of watching the ball at our own convenient rate; we can learn to *see it sooner*, and thus get a faster start on the ball as it leaves our opponent's racket; so we practice this and "strain" to see it leave the racket. This can be of particular help in the volley and return of serve situations, although it is of importance when playing on the baseline, also.

I have particularly tested this theory of mine by volleying with my players, instructing them to watch the ball leave my racket—*watch it, watch it, watch it* leave the racket. After a few minutes, when I stop and ask if this is different from what he usually does, almost always the answer is yes. Almost always he says that he normally doesn't see it leave the opponent's racket; usually he sees it "out in space" coming toward him. While being tested, however, he saw it sooner.

When teaching this on the return of serve, I want players to actually look up at the tossed ball. As a pre-test to this practice, once again players usually admit that they don't do this, that instead of looking up to see the racket meet the ball, they watch the server's total figure and then later see the ball come out of that background figure. After having been shown how to see the ball on the racket sooner—by looking up— they all agree this helps them to see it sooner. Practicing this in the beginning, many players say that the new procedure—looking up—somehow affects their timing adversely. I have found, however, that additional practice usually corrects this.

Of course, all of this relates to concentration. Concentration on what? On seeing the ball sooner, as it leaves the opponent's racket.

Preparedness is mainly a matter of mental set. Of course, be in the ready position on the line that bisects—but mainly, be mentally ready for his hit. I tell my pupils, "do as a good baseball batter does when he slips into the box; concentrate on only one thing at a time—this pitch, this shot, nothing else."

Straining to watch the ball will help them to attain this mental set.

Concentration and quick reactions, however, are not assets unless the player's ability to move for the ball is increasing—in terms of both his approach to the ball and now, most importantly, his return to position. What we are concerned with is his ability to move swiftly into a balanced hitting position and to return to a proper court position with no loss of steps beyond the ball. Improved footwork includes (1) the speeding up of the feet, (2) a balanced hitting position that encompasses *not* running past the ball, and (3) an instant return to position.

Balance, of course, remains one of our key words; now it is important to recovery.

One of the problems the intermediate faces is handling the wide shot. On the forehand, teach him to use open footwork, to slide into the shot on composition or clay, to make only a slight shoulder-turn as he runs out for the ball. On the backhand, the slide is important, but we do not suggest open footwork. We suggest underspin on both sides, and good height over the net to give him time to get back into court, a lob or semi-lob, dependent on how far he has to move beyond the sideline. The center of court may be the best spot to place these shots.

As your intermediate progresses, handling the serve becomes increasingly important. No longer can he stand there with the racket dangling at his side (did we let him do that?), and the Murphy suggestion above is most applicable on this point. In addition, we are concerned with the footwork on return of serve. The feet should be in motion just before the server hits the ball. A good way to handle this is for him to stand with the feet close together, then make a quick backward split just before the ball is hit. With the feet already started in this short, quick backward spring, your pupil will find it surprising to see how quickly he can attain proper position for hitting, once he has seen the direction of the ball.

Concentration, reactions, moving—how are they really acquired? By playing the game; by playing against players who push him to increased efforts.

A. Position Tennis

It takes a great deal of painstaking effort and attention to detail to develop proper strokes.

Work with *one* thing at time, one stroke. Often concentrating on one point at a time on one stroke is the best approach.

This principle is important on the strokes and no less important in the development of the proper tactics. Cluttering your pupils' minds with a variety of patterns of play is asking too much of them. One direction at a time is sufficient. It takes time to learn any one pattern of play well. The first important one is controlling a cross-court rally—this is position tennis.

If they know this one play and know it well, approaching it with the confidence of a player who has seen this bounce, this angle, this shot, a few thousand times before, they will be able to make it consistently.

Proper position in baseline tennis involves both the depth and width of the court. You made your beginner aware of the importance of position with the strong admonition, "stay out of No-Man's-Land," and the gentle reminder, "return to home base." In recommending that he hit balls on the descent, well back of the bounce, you set his position in relation to the depth of the court as well as the bounce. This was all your pupil needed at that point because those high-bounding balls to his opponent's backhand presumably gave him "time for a coke." Your pupil was an uninhibited pusher, and pushing tennis is a far cry from position tennis.

Now it is sheer disaster to be caught in No-Man's-Land and to leave gaps in the court. It invites well-placed balls at the feet and placements into the openings; therefore you continue to caution your intermediate player to stay out of No-Man's-Land. In addition, you will teach an entirely new concept of position tennis *in relation to the width of the court.*

To visualize this concept of position, let's consider two

13 | CHOICE OF SHOTS

players warming up for a match. Primarily, they are hitting balls back and forth to the center of court—the mechanical center of court, midway between the two sidelines. When they play, this mechanical center of court changes as they hit into one corner or the other, according to a line that bisects the angle formed by the straight and cross-court shots an opponent can make. Another way of expressing this may help: your pupil will always return to the center of an area bounded by the possible returns of his opponent.

The accompanying diagram shows this clearly.

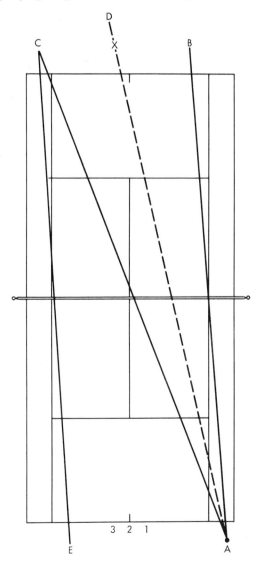

If Player A must handle a cross-court shot to his forehand beyond the right sideline, he obviously cannot hit parallel to this line. His straight shot will be AB, landing approximately two feet inside the sideline for safety. However, his position enables him to angle the ball cross-court (AC). For his opponent, the line AD that bisects these two possible shots is the center of the court. X is his home base in this playing situation.

What is the proper shot for A under this situation?

The key to baseline position tennis on both forehand and backhand sides is always cross-court. As Chet Murphy says,

Cross-courts get you out of trouble. Cross-courts keep you in the rally. Player A will have trouble getting back into position for his next shot; therefore, if he plays the ball cross-court to C, he will only have to move to position 1, a matter of two or three steps, to be on the line that bisects. If he hits to the center of court, he must return to 2; if he hits down the line, he is forced to return to 3, some four or five steps.

Chet uses another simple explanation of the importance of baseline cross-court hitting, "It's possible in a rally for a player to hit so that he doesn't have to chase wider than a sideline. If Player A hits cross-court to C, he will only have to move to E to play the ball, should his opponent elect to hit the straight shot. If he is capable of hitting the ball at a sharper angle than AC, he will take the ball inside E. On the other hand, if A elects to make the straight shot to AB, he may be driven well out of court on his backhand side."

In addition to their importance in baseline position tennis, these cross-court shots are important in percentage tennis. First of all, the net is lower at the center, the appropriate point of aim, but even more important, your player will be hitting the ball back in the same direction it comes from, rather than changing the direction with down-the-line shots which necessitate compensation for the angle of incidence.

We must constantly stress moving and reactions. Merely to know baseline position in terms of the bisecting line is not enough. The intermediate must respect it and react; he must be able to move quickly enough to be on this line, balanced, ready to move in any direction by the time his opponent hits the ball.

The application of position tennis holds two great merits for the intermediate player in this stage of his development: (1) it eliminates any questions as to *where* to hit the ball (just as it is impossible to hit a tennis ball well when he's thinking about *how* to hit it, so is it difficult to keep the errors down when there are any questions about *where* to hit it during the execution), and (2) he will play with *more consistency* because of this simple pattern. To repeat, he is not ready to maneuver his opponent, to any great extent. He is far better off making the shots he knows he can make and making them well. If he can play this simple pattern with consistency and depth, it will take a good player to beat him.

B. Playing Weaknesses

There are ramifications to this cross-court pattern, as a quote from Chet Murphy makes clear in "The Road Ahead." Once our player has become adept at playing position tennis, we will suggest modifications. Primarily they will be based on an opponent's weaknesses.

There is more to playing weaknesses than hitting to a backhand or a forehand; the weakness may be a low backhand, or a high forehand, or a wide ball, or a short one. A weakness may also be more than just a stroke—perhaps the opponent moves poorly, or moves better on one side or the other, or has a poor overhead.

One of the criteria for development from now on will be an increasing ability to play weaknesses, which calls for increasing quality of ball control. One theory of tactics holds that there is only one correct shot for every ball that is hit. This theory eliminates an opponent completely and refers only to the angles of the court. It is not a bad one, certainly. Our playing of position tennis is partially based on it, but we would like to think of our developing player as an imaginative, "thinking" player, and so we are continually offering to our intermediate some small variety in his choice of shots from the baseline as he progresses.

This in no way, however, diminishes the importance of position tennis. Varied placement comes after your pupil can control cross-court rallying.

C. Change of Pace

To perform some of the minor maneuvering that we will teach our intermediate in the final stage of his development requires a knowledge of ball speed and change of pace. Wayne Sabin explains the use of change of pace, as a concept in its own right, this way:

Ball speed may be broken down into three distinct tempos. The first is soft ball hitting; second is firm hitting, and the third is hard hitting. It might well be classified by gears, as "low gear," "second gear," and "high gear."

Soft ball, or "low gear" hitting can be very effective against a hard hitter at times in slowing down the game, or to harass and entangle a nervous, rushing player. You seldom see "low gear" tennis except, perhaps, in boys' and girls' tennis where the players have not yet reached the size or strength to do anything more effective with the ball. Certain great players, with the patience and humility required, have been able to use soft ball tactics at times to great advantage. "Bitsy" Grant, one of the great players, humbled the mightiest hitters in the world with his soft ball tactics. Even Vines and Budge, two of the greatest hitters of all time, were victims in major competition of Grant's calculated soft ball campaign. It should be pointed out that if soft ball hitting is not deep and grimly steady, it is nothing.

Firm, or "second gear," is the kind of hitting Frank Parker used. It is the kind of hitting used by almost all top players. It is the most reliable tempo with which to attain the accuracy and reliability demanded by excellent tennis. Like "low gear" hitting, "second gear" hitting must be steady and deep to be effective.

In hard hitting or "high gear," a new element enters the picture, and although steadiness is still the manifest consideration, the word *steadiness* must change to the word *percentage*. In "high gear" hitting, the great player decides to accept a certain number of errors in exchange for the disrupting influence, the havoc it will wreak on the opponent's control and equilibrium. A player must be very careful about this hard hitting. It can be deceptive because it is spectacular and more glamorous than low or second gear hitting, and if a hard hitter doesn't watch the percentages closely, he'll find that instead of beating his opponent he'll be beating himself.

Now, if a player can change gears, whether by design, or by accident, and keep the ball in court during any one point, it is an extremely disturbing factor and is referred to as "change of pace." The effect of a controlled change of pace is to disrupt the opponent's timing and groove and concentration so that he loses control. Usually, however, unless a player is very skillful and temperamentally suited to try "change of pace" tennis, instead of mixing up his opponent, he will mix himself up.

A. The Short Ball

Despite our dominant theme in this book—defense—all of us like to see and teach attack. It would be impossible, of course, not to teach it. Why? Because the short ball decrees it. It sets into action a complex of activities called volleying—pure, unadulterated attack. No matter how much we talk about defense, we love the instant reaction to the short ball, the smooth steps through the ball, the quick stop just before the opponent hits, the firm dispatch of a deep volley or the swift backward steps and the jump for the well-placed lob. This is when our player catches on fire, when his "mental set" changes from defense of the baseline to going for the kill.

To quote Bill Lufler, "The best thing that can happen is for our opponent to make an error; the next best thing is for him to hit a short ball." Using this opportunity, he says, "(1) we can use more of the court, and (2) it presents an opponent with less time." In other words, it puts him under pressure.

The short ball—the green light that says GO—may be an opponent's mistake, or part of his plan of play, or later on, something our player has created. However it happens, the meaning is the same—take off for the net!

Let's be definite about one thing—coming in is not based on the quality of your approach shot. The die is cast well before the approach shot is made; it is cast by the opponent when he hits a short ball.

But just what is a short ball?

Wayne Sabin defines the short ball as "any ball that brings your body inside the baseline to such an extent that you can't get back in time for the next shot." This is a good general definition of the short ball, but we had better give our intermediate a very restricted commitment for his first advances to the net. He is, after all, a beginner in this business of handling an approach shot and should, therefore, make

TRANSITION FROM DEFENSE TO OFFENSE | 14

his approach shots under the most favorable circumstances. Let's say, then, that he should never come in unless the ball is inside the service line, and unless it is a slow-moving ball, because a ball hit with some pace and spin may well come back to the baseline even if it lands inside the service line.

Once again, it is important to keep our pupil out of a situation he can't handle. We want to make it easy for him to have some success on his volleying venture as soon as possible; and if he comes in from too far back, he will have too little time to prepare. Therefore, he will be less likely to make a decent approach shot, and he will not get close enough to the net to be effective in his first volley, anyway. We want him to get far enough in so that he will be making his volley above the net.

B. Shaping the Approach Shot

The approach shot is not a groundstroke; it is a transportation shot, and one basic difference (whether it is hit flat or with underspin or topspin) is that the stroke is *shorter*. Both the backswing and ending are shorter. Running through the ball adds force to the shot; therefore, there is no necessity for a long backswing. The shorter ending of the stroke is dictated by these facts—we must be ready to volley immediately after the shot has been made, and we must run to the net.

Compact is the word for the technique in the approach shot.

As for the type of execution—the kinds of spin to use—there is room for considerable variety. All approach shots can be made with only minor variations of the basic concept of control that we taught to the beginner. The player can drive balls that are above the net by hitting down into them with a slightly closed racket face, or by coming up over the ball, covering it to get topspin; low balls can be hit with an open face and upward swing.

Most of us, however, prefer to see the coming-in shot handled with underspin, even some sidespin on occasions. All coming-in shots can be handled this way most satisfactorily, with the possible exception of balls above the net on the forehand side, for which we suggest the drive.

One current technique in approach is called chipping and is particularly common on the backhand side. It's a short blocking motion with underspin. Basically, it is a miniature slice and is very similar to the action on the volley.

As in everything else, you should keep a flexible attitude here and adapt the possibilities in technique to each pupil.

Regardless of how the ball is hit, this point is most important: *we move through the ball when hitting it.* We do not plod up to the ball, take a proper stance, hit the ball, look the approach shot over for quality, and then decide to come in if we like what we see. We are *always* in motion toward the net while making the approach shot.

Another basic difference that gives the approach shot a look quite unlike that of the groundstrokes is footwork. Your pupil can use *a new form* of open footwork on the approach shot. It looks like this: on the forehand, he can step into the shot with his right foot; on the backhand, with his left. This means, of course, that there is little pivot, a fact that helps to curtail the backswing. The forehand is hit with the body facing the net, the left foot coming through after or at contact. The backhand is hit with shoulders open to the net at a 45° angle, the right foot coming through the shot as the ball is contacted. This is the most acceptable method. However, there is nothing wrong in using the square stance on the forehand, with the right foot coming through with the hit, and a somewhat closed stance on the backhand, with the left foot coming in behind the right as the ball is contacted. The latter, particularly, is a preference of mine on down-the-line approach shots because it tends to prevent excessive rotation. At any rate, some flexibility will be helpful here, in view of the fact that it is not always possible for your pupil to plan ahead of time exactly how his feet will end up on a shot of this type.

If he has not had to move fast to get to the shot, he must be alerted to move fast *after he has made it* and to come to the "split stop," as Chet Murphy calls it, just before his opponent contacts the ball. Both of these points are important. There is absolutely no time for dawdling after the shot has been made (unless it has been taken very close to the net), and a player should not be moving while his opponent is making his shot. Our player must get into position soon after he makes the shot and he must be stopped, balanced on the balls of his feet. If the latter point is not included in the whole maneuver, he will find it difficult to check his direction when an opponent hits opposite to his moving.

He always moves fast after the approach shot and comes to a split stop. As a beginning volleyer, he should make his volley in a stationary position even when he has not been able to get close to the net. Later in his development, he can move through his volley, too, when he is volleying well back from the net.

But a final word of caution—there is no necessity to hit the approach hard. The approach shot is a *transportation* shot—that's all! We are using it to get in to the net, not to put the ball out of our opponent's reach. This particularly applies to the low ball.

C. Approach Placement and Net Position

We have answered one part of that question we are all asked so frequently: where should I stand at the net? The criteria for position in regard to the depth of the court is implied in our split stop just before the opponent hits the ball. We make our first volley at whatever point we have reached just

The Forehand. Note open footwork and continuous motion through the ball.

The Backhand. Note short backswing and ending and continuous motion through the ball.

before he contacts the ball. Of course, we will move from this position in the direction of the volley, if we were not close enough to the net on the first volley.

Proper position in relation to the width of the court is based on the same principle as baseline play. We take up position at the net on the line that bisects our opponent's possible shots. This means that we move *toward* our opponent when coming in, that we follow the flight of the ball. Actually, we stay a bit to the right of this bisecting line on the forehand, to the left on the backhand, to assure cutting off down-the-line shots.

This principle provides us with one definite way to place approach shots. We can play the approach shot for position—down the line off both sides. Many teachers of the game, and some of the great players, advocate this as the only coming-in shot, and it may have one definite advantage as a theory of placement in teaching beginning volleyers. As Wayne Sabin says, one of the great maxims in tennis is "Make that coming-in shot; never miss it." Missing a coming-in shot is as much a cardinal sin in tennis as double faulting or drop-shotting from the baseline. If we limit our beginner from the baseline, it follows that it may be wise to limit our beginning volleyer to placing the approach shot down the line. He practices only one thing here, as with beginning skills. In limiting him, we eliminate any questions about where to hit the ball, which can blow the coming-in shot fence high, if not sky high, in the beginning.

There are other theories and other choices for the placement of the approach shot. For instance, there is the center theory, according to which the ball is hit into the center of the court, thus cutting down the angle of return. Also, if, as some say, tennis is a game in which the offense is built into the backhand, then placement to the backhand is most important. As Bill Lufler expresses it, "You can see shots coming off the backhand quicker than you can off the forehand." It is true that the average player can attack or surprise you a little less on his backhand side, but we can always come back to our favorite gambit—playing a weakness, and in any given match, your pupil may want to play almost every shot this way.

None of these choices is as important on the approach shot, however, as this final point: if *compact* is the word for technique, *deep* is the word for placement. Deep placement is the first thing he must learn. If he does not, he might just as well run back to the baseline after he has made the shot; he has about the same chance to win the point. So concentrate on depth; choice of direction will be a simple matter later.

D. Volley Placement

Just as depth is important on the approach shot, so it is important on the first volley. It is important to keep that opponent behind the baseline. The same theories that apply in the choice of approach shots apply to the volley, also. However, it is better to allow our beginning volleyer to concentrate on one volley, the cross-court. It will be the easiest shot for him (since threading a needle with the straight volley is too difficult now); but it should be a *deep* cross-court volley, into either of the corners. He should not attempt the angled shots until later in his development.

E. The Overhead

It would be very obliging of our intermediate's opponents to let our pupil use his volley all the time in matches, but they are most likely to be contrary and want to win. And so they lob! Therefore, we must work on the overhead. Actually, we have been doing this for some time, the very minute that we started our pupil on the serve, in fact. A good overhead is a good service action; that's all it is. It is, however, complicated by two problems, the feet and judging the arc of the ball. Many pupils will have trouble attaining a consistent serve because it is difficult for them to keep their feet stationary and to control the toss. Now they are required to move their feet into a good service position underneath a ball that has been arced twenty to thirty feet in the air. It takes time to get a good overhead, and unfortunately there is not a great deal that we can teach them about it. We can tell them that a good overhead is a good service action and a million lobs away, and there *are* a few pointers that can help them.

First of all, they can shorten their backswing. Pointing the left hand at the ball as it goes up can be helpful, too, for better balance and as a reminder to watch the ball. We also suggest that when they have to go back, they move sideways and use skip steps, that they keep their feet on the ground, that they keep the head and the elbow up, that they hit the ball flat when they can, that they aim for the backhand if they can't put the ball away, that they let the short high ones bounce at first, that they hit the ball out front and hit down. There's nothing particularly earth-shaking to tell them, because those million lobs are the real answer.

Remember this, if any of your pupils think that this shot is different from the service action, or if they lose their service action taking the short swing or in moving under the ball, they'll have trouble. As in everything else on the court, rhythm is one of the basic factors on the overhead.

F. The Drop Shot

Once a player has acquired a certain amount of skill with the approach shot, he can work on the drop shot that he will occasionally use as an alternative. The drop shot is made with underspin and requires a delicate touch.

The Forehand Drop Shot.

The Backhand Drop Shot.

The racket comes from above the ball at a sharp angle and goes down the back of the ball and underneath it—a cupping effect. It should carry enough underspin to stop short. It can be used as a straight or a cross-court shot, depending on an opponent's position. It should be made with deception, because surprise is one of the most important keys to its success. There is some debate about the usefulness of a drop shot, but always remember that the more shots your pupil is able to make, the more his opponent has to worry about. Certainly, it should be used only occasionally, and there are six "nevers" you should always point out to your pupils: (1) never use it with the wind, (2) never use it on low balls, (3) never use it against speed, (4) never use it when there is lack of time, (5) never use it on the big points, and finally, (6) never, never use it from the baseline.

Now that we have moved our intermediate into an offensive pattern, we must remember that he is still basically a defensive-minded player, and if he becomes too enthralled with all the offensive possibilities, you had better bring him back to his senses with a few choice quotes from Van Horn's philosophy of defense.

(Wayne Sabin)

I divide tennis into three main areas: (1) the physical, which involves the ability to strike the ball, the ability that determines the shape of the strokes; (2) the emotional, which entails the qualities of desire and courage—the will to practice, fight, and win—and (3) the intellectual, which is the knowledge of tactics.

To be successful on the tennis court a player must possess all these attributes; unfortunately, too many players lack an understanding of the significance of the last-named area. The player who has sound strokes, desire, and courage must, in order to be a winning player, also have a mature knowledge of how the game should be played. Talent without tactics is, in the long run, chaos.

There are three things that determine how the game should be played:

1. the ABC's of tactics
2. a player's strengths and weaknesses
3. his opponent's strengths and weaknesses

I divide basic tactics into two phases. The first concerns baseline play. The very foundation of basic tactics is proficiency from the baseline.

Without an airtight, steady baseline game, the ability to defend his baseline, it is impossible for a player to use the second phase. In patrolling the baseline, the basic shots are cross-court and deep.

The first point in our ABC's is an airtight game from the baseline—deep and steady cross-court shots. No hard hitting is necessary, no great hitting. There's no need to powder the ball, but it should never be missed. However, your pupils can't win tennis matches this way. Their opponents will lose some for them, but they can't win them. What ingredients do we add for winning tennis?

THE ABC'S OF TACTICS   15

The art of winning tennis is to wait for the short ball, or, more precisely, to play in such a way that we *draw* the short ball (and this is the only excuse for any kind of stepped-up hitting—to break an opponent's rhythm or destroy his footwork, making him hit off center to give you the short ball). Then we play according to a great tennis maxim: *make that coming-in shot and that first volley and make them both deep.* Theoretically, if this is done, the point is won.

Let's picture what we are teaching here: before the short ball, both players are continually jockeying like two skilled boxers who, with left jabs, keep each other away, never hurting each other. Our players wait patiently for the opening with steady, deep cross-court play. When the short ball comes, one of them goes deep with his approach shot, deep with his volley, and the bet has changed from even to two-to-one for the man at the net.

This is the shape of the basic tactics. They are simple and exhaustible, exhaustible because there are only so many moves on a checkerboard, and simple, so simple that a player with unusual talent will feel that he should do more. That state of mind often proves to be his downfall. These ABC tactics are the letter-perfect thing to do on a tennis court, but with reservations imposed by basic laws of tennis: (1) a player should capitalize on his strength and protect his weakness; (2) he should use his opponent's weakness and rarely let him hit his strength.

We must recognize, of course, that the first phase of our basic tactics is particularly perfect for two tennis robots—two groundstrokers of giant stature with no weaknesses on either side, high, low, wide, or deep. However, our pupils do not play robots; they play human beings. Nor are they robots themselves, and so we continue to teach them to play weaknesses and, whenever possible, to hit from their strengths into their opponents' weaknesses. Certainly, we will allow the player with an outstanding flair for the game some violations of the basic tenets.

Therefore, we add this dimension beyond the basic tactics—a choice between playing cross-court position tennis and playing a weakness, which means that a player can occasionally flout his sense of sound tactics, to exploit the possibilities in the human equation. He will shed the airtight tactical patterns to take advantage of the situation of the moment. He may make wrong shots that will find his opponent completely out of position and put the ball completely out of his reach. It is the wrong shot tactically, but the right one because it is unexpected. This would be taking advantage of a strength—a big forehand, say, that could pull off this kind of play. But in the beginning, it is better to concentrate on the simple ABC's until the response is habitual and instinctive.

Wayne Sabin says of offense and defense, ". . . how hard or how softly you hit the ball has very little to do with offense or defense—rather, the issue of offense and defense is determined by your physical position on the court—and this is very simply broken down to the fact that when you play from behind the baseline (the ground game) you are in the defensive position. When you play inside the service line (the net game) you are in the offensive position."

This is an important distinction for our intermediate to keep in mind. The ability to play steady, defensive baseline tennis adds much to peace of mind. Your player will play with a sense of security if his ability to defend enables him to adopt a simple, sound offense that keeps the errors down. He must be a defensive player who knows the value of position tennis but who also knows the importance of the short ball.

His basic shots from the baseline are cross-court with an occasional down-the-line forehand, made from well inside the sideline. His basic approach shots are down-the-line.

Beyond this, your pupil can do some of the minor maneuvering we've already spoken of. He can hit short balls occasionally to bring his opponent in (because his opponent can't approach, volley, or hit an overhead). If his forehand has developed into a strength, he will be able to put a few short balls away. Finally, when he finds change of pace an important tool, he can use it. We will also show him one play at the very end of his intermediate period that will mark his progress well, showing that he is on his way to being an advanced player. It is this: in a rally, when he has made a shot that will put his opponent off balance (probably a deep cross-court forehand after his opponent has hit a down-the-line shot), we can suggest that he move in to volley the high defensive return in mid-court. (As Dennis Van der Meer says, "The ability to sense when an opponent will be off balance is one of the hallmarks of an advanced player.")

ADDING A FEW MORE POINTS 16

At long last, your pupil is in No-Man's-Land! But he is very safe, believe me. This is about all he will do, except, of course, for his tentative sallies to the net behind his serve, as we turn our back!

Much of the work that is done on the intermediate level can be placed into the general category of "helping them to find themselves." The problems that arise will be of a great variety. The most prevalent one will be making too many errors. The pupil reaches a point in his development when errors will not always be mechanical; he may be careless, not concentrating, taking his eye off the ball after four or five shots. He may be trying to take the ball too early or too late, failing to get up to it.

Perhaps he is trying to do too much to the ball, such as attempting angle shots that he's incapable of making at this stage in his development. Perhaps he is hitting too hard or trying to play "over his head" against a better player. On the other hand, he may have trouble concentrating when he plays an inferior player.

One thing that may help is for us to try to eliminate any questions in his mind as to where the ball should be hit. We want him in a positive frame of mind, always sure of himself and what he should do. And, to repeat ourselves, we want him to learn to scramble, to hustle. We want him to know the fine line between patience and aggression.

After you've seen your pupil play in a few tournaments, you'll know whether he has a nervous system that makes him tick or "tic," and if it's the latter, you'll want to help him mature into a competent match player as he goes along.

When he loses, you must analyze the loss for him. Maybe he came up against a definitely better player. Possibly he played poorly because he tried to make his shots too good. If there was little difference between the merits of the two players, then we want him to analyze what he did and why he lost. Was it playing the wrong shot? Trying to do too much with his backhand? Perhaps it was even something in the mechanics. Bill Lufler suggests the question, "If you could have done one thing better, what would it have been?" Once he knows his weakness, or weaknesses, we go right to work to help him correct them.

Lufler adds, "I want them always to ask themselves these two questions, when they are losing—'what is the other fellow doing to me, and what am I doing to keep him from doing it?' "

Condition will play an important part in his development from now on. The old Tilden theory that you get into shape for tennis by "one more set when you're tired" seems to be outmoded today. Many consider the physical training methods of the Australians one of the key reasons for their superiority in recent years. There is no question that long-distance running, sprints, jumping rope, and weight lifting are important, as well as excellent health habits. I frequently suggest some exercise, depending on individual needs. I must confess that I'm of the "old school"; I, too, like to see them "play that extra set" and work on whatever points in their game need it most.

No two tennis teachers will completely agree on exact definitions of levels of play, but most teachers agree on a general order of progression. The most difficult point at which to make a clear-cut distinction between levels is the long span between the intermediate and the advanced player, because this is where individual players swing back and forth between an intermediate's limitations and the emergence of the new and more refined capabilities of an advanced player.

This span does not include pressure tennis, as such, although your player will be coming in behind his serve more often; it is not strictly defensive tennis that includes sublety, deftness, the ultimate touch shots, but it is the beginning of the time when he will have to defend under far more difficult circumstances. The following materials by Chet Murphy, on play situations and drills to develop the skills needed, will help to bridge this hard-to-define period between the intermediate and the advanced player. These materials can be used for both intermediate and advanced players, with shifting emphasis.

A. Play Situations in Tennis

(Chet Murphy)

At any given moment in a match, a player is likely to find himself in one of several situations, depending on the tactics and strategy being used by him and by his opponent. Specifically, he may find himself in a backcourt rally exchange, or having to pass his opponent, who has just come to the net; on other occasions, our player may find himself in a position to advance to the net himself.

There are five tactical situations that may be referred to as "play situations"—(1) serving, (2) returning the serve, (3) rallying from the backcourt, (4) going to the net, and (5) playing against a man at the net. In coping with each of

THE ADVANCED
INTERMEDIATE

17

the various play situations, experienced players invariably abide by certain rules, and they follow certain specific procedures, depending on the situation. The average player would do well to plan his practice sessions and his "play for practice" so that he spends considerable time drilling on each situation. In practice he ought to adhere to the general rules and use the specific procedures that experienced players have found to be successful. Only through constant repetition can these procedures be reduced to the level of habitual response so that he acts "automatically" in any given situation. Only when he uses these procedures automatically can he use them effectively in match play. Here are the general rules, with hints and suggestions regarding the procedures, for each situation.

SERVING

In tennis it is axiomatic that you are only as good as your second serve. Therefore, practice to develop a consistent, accurate, deep second serve. Most of your second serves ought to be placed deep to your opponent's backhand; serve to his forehand often enough, however, to "keep him honest." Good depth is important on your second serve. If it is landing short, change the trajectory (the height of net clearance) by carrying the ball up on the strings more. However, your first serve offers much better preparation for a volley kill than does your second serve. Try to hit a good percentage of them in, even if it requires that you hit at less than maximum speed. Vary the placement of your first serve; serve some wide to his right, some wide to his left, and some straight at him. Try to keep him guessing and off balance. A wide serve toward the sideline will force him out of position and thus give you an opening for a volley. But serves down the middle reduce the angles he has for making returns.

Consider, therefore, the advantages and possibilities of each placement and note the trend in the match. Serving to position may, against a particular opponent, outweigh the advantage of serving to a stroke weakness. If he handles your hard serve well, it may be because he *likes* speed; in this case, stop using it; use your spin serve instead.

If you are going to the net on your serve, "get your steps." Pause and get ready to move as your opponent hits the ball. You will have to change the rhythm of your steps to correspond to the speed of your serve (two or three steps after a fast serve; four or five steps after a slower serve). If the ball is within your reach, move in for it; if it is wide, move perpendicular to it. If he suddenly moves in quickly to take your serve earlier than he usually does, make an adjustment in your steps. You must learn *always* to adjust your steps to the amount of time you have before he hits his return.

On slow courts the serve is much less effective as a preparatory shot for a volley. If he handles your serve well and is giving you trouble, it may be wise to stay back and wait for a groundstroke approach.

When you are going to the net on your serve, stand where you get the shortest line of advance to the net; if you are staying back on your serve, vary the spot from which you serve in order to get good angles on your opponent.

RETURNING THE SERVE

When you are returning the serve, the important thing is to get the return in play, not necessarily to make a winner. Stand, therefore, on the line that bisects; but consider the speed of your opponent's serve and the extent of your reach. Standing back behind the baseline gives you more time, but it also gives you a wider angle to cover.

If he consistently follows his *second* serve to the net, stand in close enough to enable you to (a) take the ball on the rise and (b) take it "high on the bounce" (above the height of the net). When you hit it cross-court, aim for the "short corner" (formed by service line and side line); when you hit it down the line, aim for either the short corner or the deep corner.

If he does not follow his serve to the net, make him go backwards to hit a backhand, except when a cross-court is necessary in order to insure getting back into position.

Make an obvious move forward as you get ready to receive his second service (it may even be a fake move). Try to tease him into taking chances.

Use your best shot (cross-court *or* down-the-line) more often than you do your uncertain shot. As a matter of tactics if you have been mixing them up, on a crucial point it may be wise to play the percentage shot; if you have been playing the percentage shot, it may be wise to mix in a surprise shot.

Learn to watch the ball leave your opponent's racket; look up to see it as he tosses it. Learn to step away from a close ball before stepping back.

If you intend to follow your return to the net, step toward the ball with the foot that is closest to the ball (the right foot, in the case of a forehand). Don't block yourself by making a cross-over step. If you intend to follow your return to the net, and he has approached behind a deep serve, the percentage shot is down the line, because it enables you to reach a good position. When you have to step sideways to reach a wide ball, step "in," perpendicular to the ball's flight.

If you are having trouble making a return, *experiment*; stand in a different place, hit the ball differently, aim to different spots.

RALLYING FROM THE BACKCOURT

Keep the ball in play; that is, don't risk an error until you have an opening. Keep the ball deep. If your opponent has a "built in" weakness, play it; if not, try to move him in order to *create* a weakness. Here again, as when serving, you must weigh the advantage of moving him against the advantage of playing his stroke weakness.

The two basic principles of baseline position play are: (1) be ready and waiting, as your opponent makes his hit, on the line that bisects the angle of the widest spots to which he can hit, and (2) when you are in trouble, place your shot to whatever spot will enable you to get back into position on the line that bisects. (Make him hit toward you; don't let him hit away from you.)

There are several tactical ways of using groundstrokes for approach shots: (1) keep your shots deep on your opponent's weak stroke until he gives you a short ball; then make an approach to his weak stroke, (2) hit wide-angled shots to move him out of position; then make an approach to either his weak stroke or where he is weak by position, (3) give him a mixture of deep and short angled shots—a mixture of shots to the deep area and to the short corners—then make an approach to where he is weak by position, (4) use the "center theory."

Control the depth of your shots by controlling the height. The height or level above the net for each shot should vary depending on the purpose of your shot and your position. To hit deeper, you may have to hit *higher* as well as harder.

When he gives you a short shot, try to get it high on the bounce so that you can hit down. Move up to the ball quickly.

Sometimes it may be necessary to play to his strong stroke in order to find an opening on his weak stroke. This occurs when he consistently runs around his backhand, for example. When you hit a strong shot to his weakness, anticipate a weak return and move up into your court a step or two, so that you will be in position to take advantage of his weak return.

Sometimes your opponent's strongest stroke is not his steadiest. His flashy, hard forehand may be more erratic than his slower, steady backhand. Consider the percentages.

When he has you running toward a sideline and you feel that you may have trouble getting into position for his next shot, hit a slow, deep cross-court. Cross-courts get you out of trouble; cross-courts keep you in the rally.

Don't be a baseline hugger. If he hits deep to you, you may have to move back to hit a groundstroke. Try to avoid having to hit a half-volley or a pick-up shot from the baseline.

Notice how he hits the ball; if he cuts it, or slices it, or spins it in any way, play the bounce accordingly.

For most effective use of the drop shot, consider three factors: (1) your distance from the net, (2) your opponent's position and distance from the net, and (3) the direction in which he is moving.

Consider the wind. When hitting against it, hit to a medium level for depth. When hitting with it, hit to a lower level. When the wind is blowing across the court, make allowance for it when aiming close to the sidelines. Certain wind conditions may give you a "downwind" shot. Maneuver your opponent and lure him into giving you a downwind shot. Drop shots and lobs will be more effective against the wind than with it.

GOING TO THE NET

Let your baseline be your guide: go to the net only when stroking from on or inside your baseline. Go to the net only when hitting *your strong stroke.* Hit it to your opponent's weak stroke, or to where he is weak by position. Make your approach shot strong enough and deep enough to force him to hit *from behind his baseline.*

Reduce to a minimum the number of errors you make on your approach shots. Don't play approach shots recklessly. Don't beat yourself; make your opponent hit good passing shots to win.

When he hits short to you, try to take the ball high on the bounce so that you don't have to hit up. You will then be able to hit hard with safety.

The best approach shots are usually down-the-line shots (either forehands or backhands), deep, but not angled.

Try to get up into the court as far as possible for your first volley. However, wherever you happen to be when your opponent strokes his shot, stop and be ready. When he strokes the ball, you should be ready and waiting on a line that bisects the angle open for his return. When he makes you hit at a low ball on your first volley, don't always try for a winner on it. It may have to be hit and placed as another approach shot. Be aware of your position when you are hitting your first volley. Are you back farther than you should be? Move up for your next volley and move toward him in the same direction.

Study his mannerisms when he strokes. Notice his stance for each kind of shot, the tilt of his racket, whether he "lines himself up" for certain shots, and so forth. These mannerisms may be giveaways of the kind of shot he intends to make and may help you anticipate it.

Anticipating defensive lobs is not difficult. It is simply a matter of putting yourself in your opponent's place; what would *you* do in a similar situation?

PLAYING AGAINST A MAN AT THE NET

Again, let the baseline be your guide: if you are hitting from inside your baseline, you may be able to pass your opponent. If you are hitting from behind your baseline, hit low so as to make him volley up; aim for a short corner. When you are very deep or on the defensive, lob!

Most of your shots against a net man should be hit into the lowest level. Make him hit at a low ball. Make him volley up. When hitting a straight down-the-line passing shot, hit it hard and deep. Aim for the deep corner.

When hitting a cross-court passing shot, hit it low with medium speed. Aim for the short corner. Hitting for the lowest part of the net (over the center-strap) may enable you to do that.

When your opponent gives you a short ball, move in quickly so that you can get it high on the bounce and thus be able to "hit down" at him.

When you are forced to hit at a short *low* ball, try to drop it at the short corner. Again, aiming at the center-strap may help.

When you make your opponent hit at a low shot, one at his feet, anticipate a weak short return. Move in so that you can take advantage of his weak return. Get it high on the bounce and pass him.

If he is at the net behind strong, deep drives, use a mixture of deep defensive lobs followed by drive returns of his smash to his feet.

Lob often enough to keep him back near his service line. Don't let him crowd the net. Your low drives will be more effective.

Keep your errors on your passing shots down to a minimum. Make him volley and smash *well* to beat you.

You have three choices: a low shot, so that he has to volley up; a winning passing shot; or a lob.

Mix them up to keep him guessing! Keep him off balance!

B. Drills for Skills

(Chet Murphy)

When planning practice schedules, most tennis coaches are faced with the same problem that confronts coaches of other sports: there just never seems to be enough time or enough space to work on all the many facets of the game. A tennis coach usually feels that there is so much to teach and so many things for his players to practice that he cannot possibly cover everything in the limited space alloted. Consequently, he must decide which of the many practice drills available to his team are needed most and which can be fitted into his schedule. To do this he must consider the level of his players and the level of their competition, and then, after considering the team's time schedule, he must select only those practice drills that will give maximum return for time spent.

This means he will have to weigh one objective against another. Specifically, for example, he will have to decide how much time to spend teaching strokes. Will he have time to change one pupil's grip, or another's habit of jumping when he hits, or a third's habit of slicing every backhand? Would it not be wiser to let them play as they do if their methods are adequate for their level and to spend most of the time teaching basic tactics and strategy so that these pupils can play effectively at their level even with deficiencies in stroke equipment?

Assuming that these decisions have been made, the coach must decide how to teach tactics and strategy that will work for his boys. At the beginning of the season he must have a preliminary plan for covering the basics. But he must also evaluate at intervals, noting the results of practice to date and the effectiveness of his players in competition. Indeed, he must even anticipate the competition and provide special drills for particular opponents.

All of this requires that the tennis coach have available on his clipboard—at his fingertips, so to speak—a list of practice drills to which he can quickly refer to meet any need as it arises. Only in this way will he be certain of providing practice procedures and routines that will enable his players to get the maximum amount of practice from the time and facilities available.

In the opening week or so of practice when the squad is working on stroke fundamentals in tossed-ball drills, as many as twelve or sixteen players can be crowded onto one court. In the bounce-and-hit feeder drills that follow, however, the number of players on one court must be reduced to as few as six or eight. Later, to provide actual rally practice or serve-and-return practice, the number must be reduced even more. Provision must be made for the singles players to practice the kind and sequence of shots used in match play.

Usually, by providing stations at which players can practice various skills (each court can be one station for one specific drill) and by having the boys rotate from station to station, a coach can arrange to cover most of the basics and even many of the "specials" he has devised for specific players and for specific opponents. Eight or ten boys can be practicing strokes on one court, for example, while at the same time, two, three, or four boys can be practicing some point of tactics on another court. With careful planning of this kind, the coach can quickly bring his more advanced boys to the point where they are ready for intensive work in game-like conditions. Some coaches feel that this is best done in actual play, but many prefer to break the total game down into small units in which various "specifics" of tactics can be practiced separately.

The remainder of this discussion is devoted to descriptions of several such units used by many experienced coaches in their team practice sessions. For convenience, each one is given a descriptive name. Players soon learn the names for each and quickly change from one to another as the coach suggests.

MOVING YOUR MAN

Both men rallying from the baseline (no net play allowed).
Used effectively as a warm-up because it prevents players from hitting

carelessly. One player is told to "move" the other, by placing his cross-court and down-the-line shots as best he can. The other player retrieves and practices defensive shots and playing for recovery into position. The coach can stress form on groundstrokes and position play. After five or six minutes, players change assignments.

THE DEEP GAME

Both players rallying from baseline.

Mark off a "deep area." Players start rally with a bounce-and-hit, and rally from the backcourt, each trying to hit into the deep area. After they have done this drill on several successive days, have them stop the rally if the ball doesn't land in deep area. Later, let them continue the rally even on a short ball; let the first man who gets a short ball go to the net. Still later, let players begin each point with a serve and actually keep score. But here again, have them stop the rally if a ball lands short of the deep area. (At this point, emphasize the deep return of serve that makes the server go backwards to hit a backhand).

NO SERVE TENNIS

Player starts rally from backcourt with a bounce-and-hit.

The serve and return of serve are often used as cover-ups by players as explanations of their bad play. To prevent this and point out the importance of, and their lack of, ability in baseline play, have players play and keep score without serving. Here, the "server" starts with a bounce-and-hit and immediately tries to hit deeply enough to keep his opponent on the defensive. Play continues in normal manner.

THREE-SHOT TENNIS

In all but the exceptionally good school play, players who try to play the all-court game are known to miss most often on three shots: the approach shot, the first attempt to pass, and the first volley. This drill provides practice in nothing more than those three shots. One player makes a bounce-and-hit from the baseline and runs to the net to volley. The other player returns as best he can, and the first player attempts to make his volley. To emphasize the importance of keeping the ball in play on these three shots, instruct the player to hit easily and to hit directly to the opponent. You'll probably find both of them missing one of the first three shots even under these easy conditions. Later, as a player gets better, let him hit away from his opponent and yet emphasize keeping the ball in play and winning the three-shot game.

SERVE AND DEEP RETURN

Mark off a deep area. Server serves in regular manner and receiver tries to return to deep area. He wins point if he does; he loses point if he doesn't. No rallies allowed; emphasis is on serving effectively enough to bring a short return and on returning deep enough to keep the server on the defensive.

SERVE AND SHORT RETURN

Server serves in regular manner. Receiver tries to return to short area, inside the service line (as he would if server were coming to the net). No rallies allowed. Receiver wins point if he returns short. Server tries to win point by serving effectively enough to prevent receiver from making a short return. When players are too good for this simple version, extend a string across the net and make the return man hit under the string.

SERVE AND FIRST VOLLEY

Server serves in regular manner and dashes to net for a volley. Receiver returns as best he can. No rallies allowed at first in order to focus attention on the return of serve. Later, let players play the point out without keeping score. In this practice, stress doing what they cannot do well.

VOLLEYING THROUGH MID-COURT

Two players stand on baseline at opposite sides of the court. Either starts a rally with a bounce-and-hit, and moves up *two steps* after his hit. Second player returns and moves up *two steps*. Rally continues with each player moving up two steps after each hit. They try to keep the ball low, at the opponent's feet, to make him hit up. They try to work their way in to the net with low shots at the feet of the opponent so that they can get the first chance to hit hard and down for a winner.

PASSING SHOTS—ONE AGAINST TWO

Place two volleyers at the service line, one on each side of the center service line, about a half step from the line. One player on the far side of the net at the baseline tries to pass the two net men. He aims for the short corners, and plays out every shot as if it were a point in a match. Volleyers practice making the proper moves, a cross-over step. Passer studies his hits so that he soon learns his strong shots. In a match, he ought to use his best pass shot much more often than his risky one, and always on a crucial point. Net men are reminded to analyze the pass shots and try to figure the passer's best shots.

VOLLEYS—ONE AGAINST TWO

One volleyer volleys to either of two backcourt men. Purpose is to give the volleyer practice at angling his shots and getting used to angled balls coming at him.

VOLLEYING FOR QUICKNESS

Two players play at the net, volleying "faster than they can do it." Emphasis is on speed volleying.

MAKING THE FIRST VOLLEY

Volleyer stands at the service line and returns from there as he would on his first volley in match play. Either of two baseliners try to pass him.

LOBS AND SMASHES

Two baseliners lob to a net man. Later, baseliners mix lobs and drives. They try to push him back with a lob so that they can drive at his feet, and even take the net away from him.

PART

IV

The Advanced Player

A. Ball Control and Advanced Tactics

At the beginning of the book we stressed that the lessons of the present are as important as lessons of the past. Modern tennis has made us more conscious of playing on different surfaces and taught us the importance of developing a big serve.

Now at long last, we're ready for the Big Game—attack. Whereas once we told our pupils all about Bobby Riggs (and how we loved to talk about him!), *now* we can tell them all about Jack Kramer and Gonzales (always, however, continuing to speak of Budge in hushed, reverent tones). Why the Big Game only *now*, after all these years? A quick look back at Chapter 2, "A Framework for Teaching," and a review of the criteria outlined there for our advanced player will remind you that *pressure* tennis is his strategical framework.

First, what is the heart of pressure tennis? Coming in behind the serve, of course, (yes, we do want them to do this now, with certain restrictions that we will note later), but the big serve is only part of the Big Game. Pressure tennis encompasses ball speed (how that will increase for your pupil within the next few years!), taking the ball on the rise and farther in front of the body. The fact that your pupil will be playing close to the baseline will enable him to handle that increasingly longer "short ball." It will enable him to use more and more of his opponent's court and to counterpunch, also. Further, his volleying will have reached the point at which he will be at home in No-Man's-Land. All of this spells *pressure*, because it will keep his opponent out of position and off balance.

Yes, the accent is on attack, at last. This emphasis, however, must not be allowed to diminish our interest in increasing our pupil's ability to defend.

What if his opponent is also playing the Big Game? If we draw a picture of the patterns of play on this advanced

THE STRATEGICAL FRAMEWORK

18

level, we will find that our pupil is a many-faceted player. He is subjected to just about every test there is on a tennis court, and he himself now causes a few things to happen. If we place all his skills under the two categories, defense and offense, we will realize that he must be able to defend against the same offensive moves that he can make because his opponent is, theoretically, about the same kind of player. Each can do what the other can do; in other words, winning depends on how well he can do them.

In a sense we are setting up a theoretical match; not an offensive player against a defensive player, but a match in which the tides turn from defense to offense to defense, depending on the strengths, weaknesses, and mistakes of each player. This is the relativity that exists in tennis.

If our player is a good defender, just how good is he against an excellent attacker? If he is a good attacker, just how good is he against a good defender? What we mean by "the more complex rhythms of the game" is that the playing situations our pupil finds himself in change faster now. For every playing situation that he forces his opponent into, he will be forced into the same or a similar situation by his opponent.

He must be a defender as well as an attacker, so the finishing touches on the advanced level will include far more than attack; they will include touch on all of the delicate shots, the development of the offensive lob, and the extensive use of underspin (because he has less time and because he is hitting the ball on the rise). We will be working toward having the player use all the degrees of spin called for in all the varied playing situations. He will need variety in the shape of the strokes that will enable him to use the right spin at the right time. We now may want him to be able to come over his backhand and to use underspin on the forehand more frequently. Now more than ever, spin becomes important in relation to tactics. But all these goals are modified by our assumption that tennis games are tailor-made.

The very sound "ABC's of Tactics" by Wayne Sabin is a far broader view of patterns of play than one might notice on first reading. "Capitalizing on a strength and using an opponent's weakness" makes room for every kind of player, every way of playing the game. It includes the big serve of a Doeg, the Big Game of a Kramer, the ball control of a Bobby Riggs, or the lightning reactions of an Henri Cochet. It includes all kinds of baseliners, all kinds of net rushers. From this one statement we see clearly how individual differences become an asset and shape the style of a player's game. As individual differences appear, we take them into account. Whereas in the past they have been limited to the shapes of the strokes, now they include playing patterns and strengths in stroking equipment.

Now we can see something emerging: the possibility of a fine defensive game, a groundstroke power, a big serve, or a great net game. Depending on all the player's weaknesses and strengths and all of his physical, mental, and emotional attributes we will make our plans, encouraging the player always to use his strengths, whatever they are, but continuing to work with him on his weaknesses.

It is on the advanced level that the differences in playing surfaces, in addition to individual differences, most influence the playing of the game.

B. Percentage Tennis on Different Surfaces

(Bill Lufler)

KINDS OF SURFACES

There are almost as many different tennis court surfaces as there are countries. However, for the purpose of this discussion, we shall use general classifications. Well over 90 per cent of the courts in the world are of clay, or of a surface so comparable to clay that they can be grouped under this heading. Throughout Europe, for example, one may look a long time before discovering any other type of outdoor court surface.

The game was first played on grass, and although the number of grass courts equals but a fraction of the total number of clay courts, the great championships of the game are still competed for on grass surfaces. England, the home of the game, has its All-England Championships at Wimbledon. Played on grass, this is the greatest of all the championships and the most coveted of all tennis titles. The United States Championships, played at the West Side Tennis Club at Forest Hills (perhaps the most important championship after Wimbledon), is also played on grass. That great tennis country Australia holds its championships on grass. So, although millions of tennis players never hit a ball on a grass court, grass is still the surface of the great championships. For the most part, grass courts are to be found in England, on the Eastern seaboard of the United States, and in Australia. India has some grass courts, and there are other scattered grass court centers, but they are few.

Cement courts are found mostly in America, and in the state of California in particular, one must look for a court other than cement just as long as one must look for other than a claylike court in Europe.

Certain sections of Europe, notably Sweden, possess many indoor courts with a wood surface. These, then, are the four major divisions of court surfaces: clay, grass, cement, and wood. There are varieties of all four, and we shall touch on them now.

Because they are many times more numerous than all other surfaces combined, let us first consider the clay, or claylike, surface. During the first few of my teaching years in Europe, I would refer from time to time to "clay" courts; invariably, there would be a slight pause in the conversation and some clarification needed from me. I soon stopped using the term altogether, although every single outdoor court upon which I played throughout Europe fell definitely within this category as we would define it. Almost from the beginning of tennis on the Continent, the standard or popular court has carried the name of its maker. What this maker produced was a gritty-like top dressing for courts. It was usually dark red in color, which made it most pleasant to the eye and served as a fine background. This top dressing, or court surface, was quite porous and was applied on top of a carefully installed foundation which allowed quick drainage. These were, and are, generally referred to as "fast drying" or "quick drying" courts, and play is possible within a very short time following even the heaviest of rainfalls. There are many such top dressings on the market today, and they usually bear the name of the manufacturer. There are thousands of installations of courts in this country that fall definitely within our term of "clay" courts. In fact, the United States National Clay Court Championships are played on exactly such courts. Their advantages lie in the fact that they drain much more quickly than clay, and as a rule the maintenance required is much less than for clay.

These courts are seen more often in this country in a green color, while Europe still seems to prefer the dark red. Sometimes the top dressing is applied on top of a clay court in this country, simply to add color to the court. The color and substance of clay vary in different sections, and so do clay courts. Some clays are light in color, and others are quite dark. Some may be more dirt than clay.

It is on grass, perhaps, that the full range of tennis skill can best be employed. That is true, of course, if the grass is good. Grass courts, like clay courts, can vary quite a bit. One thing that does not vary is the fact that grass is very expensive to keep in condition. In my opinion, the quality of grass courts has declined somewhat in recent years. Grass courts need not only extensive and almost continuous care, but also the right climate. This is one reason that for years grass courts have been mostly limited to England, Australia, and the Eastern seaboard of the United States. All these areas are near water or have a damp climate. The type of grass used, the cutting of it, the weight of the rollers used on it, and, of course, the amount of play all contribute to the playing qualities of grass. The name of the game is "Lawn Tennis," and it is interesting to note that some of the original tennis centers are still the big centers and are still using grass.

For some years, cement courts were to be found only in California. Recently, court construction companies have found that by far the greatest demand has been for this type of court. There are several reasons for this; perhaps one of the leading reasons is economy. Once a cement court has been installed, the only upkeep required is brushing the court clear of dirt and occasionally repainting the lines or restaining the surface. In these days of soaring labor costs, the maintenance problem has become an acute one.

The tennis court engineers have also come up with some new surfaces that fall within the cement category but include some added features. Each company seems to have its own name or names for these surfaces, but they are quite alike in that they have produced a solid-surfaced court with some "give" and "spring." They are a bit easier on the feet and legs than cement. They are available in different colors, with green and red being most popular. Some are stained after the surface has set. They are usually playable soon after a rain and need only a brushing to make them ready for play.

The use of wooden courts has been quite extensive in tennis-loving Sweden and, to a much lesser extent, in other countries where long and hard winters are the rule. These courts also vary, but less than some of the other surfaces. Wooden courts may be found with canvas stretched over the surface. Lately, other surfaces have come along that can be installed over the wood itself. There are some wooden courts in the northern sections of the United States.

So, we have four general classifications of courts. Let us next turn to the playing qualities of the various surfaces and then to methods of play that best suit each surface.

PLAYING QUALITIES OF THE VARIOUS SURFACES

There can be no real comprehension of the playing qualities of the various surfaces or how best to play on the various surfaces without an understanding of one all-important fact: some court surfaces play "fast" and some play "slow." A great majority of players misunderstand completely what is meant by this. In what manner is it judged that a certain court possesses fast or slow playing qualities? What exactly is the gauge of measurement?

It is of utmost importance, as a basis for an understanding of this entire matter, to know the amount of time that elapses between the moment the ball meets the court the first time and the moment it hits, or would hit if allowed to bounce again, the second time. That period of time is the time one has in which to reach and hit the ball. The longer this period of time, the slower the game, and, conversely, the shorter this period of time, the faster the game. Let us see how the surfaces we have discussed vary with regard to this time element.

Grass—beautiful green grass, so pleasant and so soft to the feet—invariably misleads the uninitiated. It is a very fast surface indeed. Why? Because the ball doesn't rise a great deal from the surface, and one has a minimum of time to reach the ball and execute the necessary stroke. Clay is almost the opposite. The ball bounces up, its forward speed slowed more by contact with the surface than it would be with grass, and one has much more time in which to reach the ball and make the necessary stroke. Cement lies somewhere in between these two. The ball is not slowed appreciably by contact with cement, but it bounces much higher than it does on grass. Cement is definitely a fast surface, however. Wood is at the end of the scale, the extreme opposite of clay, and the fastest surface of all. The ball skids on contact with the surface, and the player has the absolute minimum of time in which to move to the ball. There, in bare outline, are the general characteristics of the most common court surfaces.

These four general divisions of court surfaces can be further broken down, because each class may vary considerably. These variations can be caused by climatic conditions, court maintenance, court construction, and so on. Grass varies a great deal, even at clubs in the same geographical area. Different types of grass or combinations can be used. Some grass courts are kept close-cropped and are heavily rolled. Others are maintained in an entirely different manner because of differences in grass types. Local conditions, such as the amount of rainfall, presence of certain fungi, or even the preference of various groundsmen or club officials, affect the grass. The differences between the courts at such world-famous clubs as Wimbledon's All-England Club and Forest Hills' West Side Tennis Club are quite pronounced. Clay courts have many variations, too. Extremes might be a sun-baked clay court in the midwestern United States and a fast-drying court in France. The ball bounces high on sun-baked clay, and much lower on the fast-drying type. The latter sometimes gives the impression that the ball is almost hanging in the air, so much does the surface check the bounce. In any event, on clay one has a bit more of that so precious ingredient—time.

One wouldn't usually think of variations in cement court surfaces, but for some time two of California's biggest tournaments were played within a week of each other and on courts that varied a great deal as to speed. The reason can be found in the method of finishing the cement surface. A smooth-finished cement is faster than a cement finished with certain whorls or a degree of coarseness.

HOW TO PLAY THE VARIOUS SURFACES

Great players can win on all types of surface. However, it does not follow that these great players have been equally at home on all surfaces. Rather, they have become great because of their ability to adjust their games to the problems various surfaces present, as well as to the problems posed by their opponents.

I have known many good players, just a peg or so below the top, who act as if all surfaces are the same, never varying their game regardless of the surface. They can be heard complaining bitterly about clay being too slow and grass too fast. In all sports, and tennis is by no means an exception, playing the percentages is an accepted way of life. Percentages can apply to points, to shots within these points, choice of shots, and so forth. The player who fully grasps the game reacts to such situations and is able to play percentage tennis. Playing the surface is certainly a major—and obvious—consideration in percentage tennis. Unfortunately, it is often not so obvious.

Let us try to visualize four courts: one of grass, one of clay, one of cement, and one of wood. We will move from one to another to make a few points about playing the various surfaces and playing percentage tennis by doing so.

Let's go first to the grass court:

Here are two fine players, both rather completely equipped as to strokes. Both are good fighters, and both concentrate well. Physically, one is quite a bit larger and more powerful than the other. This more powerful player has a big serve and more weight of shot than the other. He is not blessed with great mobility, but neither is he exactly a slowpoke, although his opponent is much quicker about the court.

What do we see? The big player is serving and following in to the net position behind each serve. His serve is coming off the fast court like a shot. It is earning points directly, and it is forcing some high returns by sheer power and speed of the ball. He is dealing decisively with these high returns and in general is enjoying a definite margin of superiority when serving.

We ask them to move over to the next court, the clay court. The same man serves, and follows it in, as on grass. Now, what do we see?

We see the big serve, still not easy to take, but bouncing higher and much more slowly after contact with the clay surface. Now, the receiver, with a shade more time to react and to pick his shots, is not only directing them more accurately, but is also keeping them much lower. He may not be turning back the big serve with one shot, but he is invariably putting the ball in play and often forcing the server to volley from below the height of the net. No longer does the server have a routine high volley to knock away; he is presented with low volleys, from which he must make difficult shots or be left in a most distressing position for the next shot by his opponent.

This is, I admit, a most simple and obvious example, but it does point out how the slower court can help a player who is almost overwhelmed by the power of his opponent's serve on a fast court. That extra split second in which to react and to catch up with that old ball—the time element!

Let us continue with the same pair of players. We move to the wooden court, and the big server's eyes light up again, as indeed they should. His serve again is devastating, even more so than on grass.

We make a final move and this time find ourselves on cement. Here the odds swing back again a bit toward the receiver. This does not mean that on any of these surfaces the receiver has the advantage over the server, but the server's superiority does vary with the surface. The service comes off fast on cement, but is bouncing up higher than on grass, so that the receiver is able to hit downward at the ball and does have a fraction more time than he does on grass or wood, although not as much as he does on clay. Time, wonderful time, and he has more choice of shot because of it and the slightly higher bounce found on clay and on good cement.

Here we have the effect of the various court surfaces on the server and the receiver. Do not draw the conclusion that the server wins almost automatically on grass nor that the server is almost at the mercy of the receiver on slow clay. However, all else being equal, it hardly takes an expert to sense the increased advantage held by the server as the court surface becomes faster. So, on the fast surfaces, we see the server take advantage of his opportunity by coming in behind his serve almost every time. He is playing percentage tennis. He is doing exactly the same thing, playing the surface, and by doing so, playing the percentages, by coming in less often and less directly when on slow courts.

Let's take another example of playing the surface. Again we will start off with a grass court. A rally is in progress, and one of the players has been attacked by a wide ball to his backhand, which his opponent has followed to the net. He can reach the ball, but is moving rather fast when he gets there. He aims close to a line and goes for a clean passing shot. He realizes he is moving so fast that he must go past the spot where he meets the ball, and he knows he cannot get back for the volley, anyway. So he hits it! He goes for the outright winner.

Visualize the same situation on a fast-drying, claylike court. Our player may still go for a clean pass, but the chances are that he will get to the same attacking shot a shade earlier. The ball's forward speed has been checked by the surface, and in addition the player is able to slide into his shot and is not forced to run past his shot as he must on fast courts. He will have more time to control the ball, and he will be able to regain position much more quickly. He can afford not to go for a clean passing shot unless he believes the odds are in his favor, and he can concentrate on keeping the ball low to his attacker at the net. If he succeeds in this, he will have a good chance to run down the ensuing volley, and many times on slow courts, the second stroke against a net player is much more damaging than the first.

Innumerable examples of this kind might be given. Club players of average ability can sometimes improve their games considerably, not by working on changes or adjustments in strokes, but by choosing shots well.

In any event, one may be able to get an idea here of just why the tennis being played by practically the same players can vary so much on different surfaces. On the slower courts, it is more difficult to put the ball away, as the opponent has more time. Therefore, one must hit harder and take more chances to get the same result on slow courts as on the faster ones. This usually results in more errors, of course, so playing the percentages, the players must work for an opening and wait for an opening, until the opportunity, which comes more quickly on fast courts, is at hand.

Only the absolutely best, and not always these, can attack continually on the first stroke on slow courts. For that reason, many players prefer the slower courts. The points develop more slowly; there is more variation of stroke and tactics, and so on.

Of course, we have the extremes: two brawny heavy servers with not much else, except adequate volleys and a smash, can certainly put on a rather boring display when matched on a very fast court. One yearns for the clever baseliner who might conceivably put a ball in play off service occasionally and might even feel the compulsion to hoist up a lob once in a while. At the other extreme: is there anything more boring to witness than a long five-setter (equally unimaginative tennis) on slow courts with neither player willing to employ pace or to force the play unless presented with a shot that brings him almost to the net itself? Here one yearns for the big serve and the unanswerable smash. But, extreme or not, that's the game!

Here are a few added thoughts:

Many players find it easier to attack cross-court on clay than on grass, because the ball bounces higher and thus exposes more angles into the opposite court. Drop shots are employed more often on slow courts than on fast, although drop volleys are used with some effect on grass. As a rule, the faster the server, the more effective the serve on fast courts. On return of service, the slow courts give more time and give a higher bounce, which offers more range of return. Some players rarely try to pass cleanly on slow courts unless absolutely certain of the odds, and try to put their attacker in difficulties by low or wide balls, with the idea that they can then run down these difficult volleys and often be in a more advantageous position than when hitting the preceding stroke. These are very good tactics on return of service on slow courts. Some champions are able to employ these tactics on grass, except from all but the best serves, but then are faced with that old bugaboo—the time element—on the next shot. In addition, the ball will be lower on grass than on clay, and they will again be hitting up to the volleyer. Along this same line, I know of several top players who, for this reason, almost invariably go for a winner on return of service when playing on fast courts. Against all but the best serves, they feel that they may have a better chance on the return of serve than after the server makes his first volley.

The lob, most neglected of all shots in the modern game, can be used on all surfaces. The smash, somewhat like the service, is easier to put away on fast courts, so the lobs must be better on fast courts than on clay.

None of this should be construed to mean that only those with the big serves and the Big Game can win on grass or that the clever baseliner will automatically give these Big Game boys a thorough trouncing on slow courts. It *does* mean that players should alter their tactics to allow for the surface upon which they are to play.

Players referred to as "hitters" have won such great titles as the French

Championships on the very slow courts of Paris, while some referred to as "baseliners" have triumphed on the fast grass at Wimbledon and Forest Hills. However, none have triumphed without some adjustment of their game to the surface on which they were playing. It is the mark of the great players, this ability to adjust and to win the "big ones," on all surfaces.

Club players, college players, and all those who play competitive tennis will enjoy this great game the more for having an understanding of the various court surfaces and the demands these surfaces make on the players.

A. The Final Shaping of the Strokes

THE ADVANCED SERVE

There are certain teaching tasks that particularly challenge the imagination and patience of the tennis instructor. The development of the advanced serve is one of these, and the many facets of this particular challenge make it a fascinating task.

In describing the beginners' serve, Welby Van Horn said, "Of all the strokes in tennis, the serve . . . is the most difficult to *perfect*. The final shaping of the stroke as used by championship players bears little resemblance to the initial shaping of the stroke that beginners should use." But there is more involved in the challenge than mechanical details that shape the advanced serve. There is more variety of choices in every part of the serve than in any of the other strokes, and in addition, our expectations of the serve at this point are extremely high. Let's discuss these three phases of the challenge, adding to our total picture of the advanced serve as we do so.

Technically there is a considerable way to go between the intermediate serve and the championship swing if we have followed closely the slow but sure steps that Van Horn outlines from the beginning to the end of the development of the serve. Here are the specific changes we will make for the advanced serve:

1. The grip is now Continental.
2. The two arms are completely synchronized in the windup and the toss.
3. The forward weight distribution begins earlier; the weight starts forward with the toss.
4. The ball is tossed farther back. (This and the grip change result in a more definite *pulling* motion.)
5. There is a greater rotation of the body in the backswing.

THE TRANSITIONAL
STAGE

19

(At the end of the backswing, the back is bent around, not down, so that the server would fall into court if pushed. The back is slightly arched.)

6. The racket makes a full loop now in the "scratching the back" motion.
7. There is a greater drop of the left shoulder as the ball is hit.
8. The right foot comes over after the hit.

Depending on the pupil, any *one* of these changes may keep his instructor busy for some time. One pupil may run into considerable trouble with the grip change. The full service grip (the Continental grip) provides the maximum in wrist action for both power and spin, but will often be a loss of power and a loss of control when the change is first made. Again, changing the weight distribution and adding greater rotation of the body will tend to disturb the toss and the rhythm. The inability to execute the loop properly may be one of the most common faults in the serve.

The challenge of developing the championship serve is further complicated for the instructor because of the many possibilities in each part of the serve. There may be slightly different stances, broad differences in where racket and ball start, and broad differences in the windup. There are a variety of weight shifts, of rhythms, and different tosses in terms of height and placement. Some serves look like pulls, others like hits. The variety of styles suggests that serves, like the groundstrokes, are tailor-made, that individual differences must be allowed here as elsewhere in the game.

Finally, we see the challenge fully crystallized in the *uses* of the advanced serve:

1. to hit to a weakness
2. to hit with enough speed to provoke a weak return
3. to pull an opponent out of court
4. to come in behind

Accuracy, power, spin, and net attack—this is what we expect of the advanced serve, and we must select, from the many options, the right combination that provides a look of synchronization between the toss and racket swing, a coordinated look of precision as though the server were measuring the height he wanted the toss to have with his left hand and then measuring that toss with his racket. We must get a balanced look in everything from stance to finish, as the racket moves in a continuous, whip-like swing that is rhythmically grooved and capable of repeating the same motion to the same toss over and over again.

The same toss to the same swing, the same rhythm to the same balance: this spells accuracy if we serve with some spin—and remember, final accuracy means 70 per cent of first serves in and *no* double faults.

However, accuracy alone is too little to expect at this point. We want power when we can get it, power that comes from an accelerated racket swing that enables the racket to reach its maximum speed at point of impact. This involves a windup that places the body in a coiled position at the end of the backswing, and then an unleashing of this potential energy through the straightening of the arched back and the knees, the full upward uncoiling of the body, and finally, a strong forearm action and wrist snap. We want enough power to provoke the weak return, and we want that occasional ace on the fast surfaces.

We want the serve grooved, yes, but with enough flexibility in the swing to utilize all of the spins—sidespin (slice), overspin, and even, possibly, the American Twist if we can combine it with enough speed. Only with spin can we serve safely to open the court for the first groundstroke or volley. Yes, for the first volley, too, because the serve is now a full-force attacking weapon that can be followed to the net. Use of the serve involves our main goal for our advanced player. On the fast surfaces he will put pressure on his opponent by coming in behind his serve.

It is obvious that the final shaping of the advanced serve takes considerable time, effort, and patience. It also requires constant review, detailed explanations of the various parts of the serve, and corrective techniques.

Let's now break the details of the serve into six parts—the stance, the toss and backswing, the loop, the forward swing, the hitting area, and the finish.

The Stance: It should be taken one to two feet from the center line. The feet are about a shoulders' width apart. The toes are lined up in the direction of the flight of the ball. This means a straight or slightly open stance when the player is serving into the right court, a slightly closed stance for the left court. The left foot makes a 45-degree angle with the baseline, one or two inches from it. The weight is on the right foot; the heel of the left foot is off the ground; the body is approximately sideways to the net. The racket is held above the waist and is cradled at the throat by the left hand.

The 45-degree angle, one or two inches from the baseline, is important because it will tend to eliminate foot-faulting. Further, as the player comes up into the serve, he pivots (or rotates) on the ball of the left foot, and the 45-degree angle facilitates this rotation. The serve should be made over the left foot, which should not leave the ground nor move forward at any time during the serve. It will be noted, however, that many of today's championship players do jump off the ground with a "scissors kick" when they serve. Some of them serve so well doing this, who can say it is wrong? It is, of course, an outgrowth of the modern net-rushing game and may facilitate getting to the net; however, it should be carefully avoided if possible. The advanced server should continue to serve with the left foot contacting the court throughout the serve, and if later he develops a scissors kick from rushing the net, the criteria for using it are these: he should still be getting 70 per cent of his first serves in, and he should never double-fault.

As we noted earlier, there can be many acceptable alternatives to the stance as outlined here. The weight can rest on the left foot or be evenly distributed. In both cases, however, it would be shifted to the right foot in the beginning of the windup. If the player finds a slight rocking motion helpful to his rhythm, let him use it. Also, racket and balls can start down and come up *together*. The main object here is whatever is natural, and comfortable—whatever looks and feels rhythmic from the start.

The Toss and Backswing: The racket head and ball begin the serve simultaneously. Both drop down together. The ball stops at the mid-waist point, and pauses for a bare fraction of a second while the racket continues to go down past the right foot. As the racket starts its upward motion, the left hand tosses the ball upward. The ball is always held between two fingers and the thumb. The arm is slightly bent at the beginning of the toss and straightens out as the ball goes up. The word "toss" may be a misnomer in this case. The ball is *placed* in position, actually, with more of a thrusting motion than a toss. One good image is that of thrusting the ball up through a slotted stovepipe, the hand starting at the bottom of the stovepipe about mid-waist and going straight up. The placement of the ball depends on the type of serve desired—slice, flat, topspin, or American Twist. With the toss varying from right to left, the toss should be to the far right for the slice serve, and we hit on the outside of the ball and around it. The ball is tossed progressively more to the left for the three remaining serves—straight ahead for the flat serve (the hand snaps the racket head perpendicular to the ball's line of flight); somewhat in line with the head for the overspin serve (the hit is more up and over the ball) and finally, even farther to the left for the American Twist, with the racket snapping up over the ball and from left to right, although eventually it is nice to think of the deception that can come from hitting all four of these serves off the same toss. The ball should be thrown about a foot or so in front of the baseline and as high as point of contact, although some players time their swing to a ball tossed one or two feet above this point.

While the toss is being made, the racket drops down past the right foot. It reaches the end of the backswing with the arm comfortably extended. The racket head is higher than the wrist and perpendicular to the playing surface. The upper part of the arm is approximately parallel with the court surface (the elbow is shoulder height or just a bit lower). During the toss and backswing, this is the action of the body: the weight transfer begins with the toss; it is not particularly noticeable, however, because as the weight is shifted, the body rotates (the right shoulder turns backward). The back is slightly arched, and the knees are bent.

Alternatives should be noted here, also. Some players do not bring the ball down at all; others bring it down until it almost touches the left leg. Again, the tendency today is to shorten the swing I have described, to sweep it upward in a somewhat outward arc. In this type of backswing, the racket may never drop below the waist. All these alternatives are permissible. The key is to experiment until the synchronized, rhythmic look is there.

The Loop: The loop begins at the end of the backswing. It can be referred to as a dip and a whip. What takes place is this: the racket continues its upward arc; up to this point there has been little action of the wrist, but now the wrist comes into action and this action is coupled with a sharp break in the elbow; after the peak of the upward arc, the racket dips down the back to perform the "scratching the back" motion; the racket then whips out to a position well behind the ball. This very full loop may be the one most difficult part of the serve. We could say that the serve begins at the end of the backswing. Up to this point, we have merely tossed the ball up and swung the racket back in preparation for this loop action and the forward swing. It is in the loop that the racket really begins to pick up speed, accelerating to its peak at point of contact. If this loop action is restrained or curtailed in speed of racket or size of loop, power will be lacking. There is wrist, yes, but just as important is a strong shoulder and elbow action. It is the right shoulder and elbow rotating around into the hit that enables the racket to whip out to a point well behind the ball.

The Forward Swing: At this point, we are justified in comparing the service action to that of a baseball pitcher. Pictures of pitchers pitching (try that one on a pupil at the end of a long day!) show how the elbow leads, followed by a strong upward forearm action, and finally, the wrist snap. Lester Stoefen, one of the outstanding teachers of the serve, says, "The hand triggers the serve." This is an apt expression for the final control and power on the serve. The particular slant or bend of the racket is controlled by the hand or wrist.

The Hitting Area: Yes, there is a hitting area on the serve as well as on the groundstrokes, particularly on the flat and overspin serves (somewhat less on the slice and the American twist because the racket is going out around the ball and across the ball, respectively). The action on all four serves is *outward* as much as possible. The more the shoulder allows the racket to go out on the ball, the better. The action in the hitting area is best described as "up, over and out." The concept "carry" applies here as well as on the groundstrokes. Actually, what we are doing here, from the end of the loop, is *throwing* the racket through the hitting area.

The Finish: This will vary according to the type of serve. The slice will end well to the left, with the contact side of the face pointing slightly upward. The flat serve will end to the left, with the contact side pointing slightly downward. The overspin serve ends approximately in front of the server. The American Twist ends to the left also; it is a *fallacy* to think that the American Twist has to end to the right behind the server.

The development of the advanced serve calls for considerable use of corrective techniques. One such technique is the use of the ultimate in short backswings—the one that comes up and around directly from the toss—to correct a low elbow at the end of the backswing or to increase the size of the loop (here we are referring to that part of the loop that occurs after the "scratching the back" action, the part that finds the racket whipping out from the back to a position well behind the ball). Another technique to correct both this javelin-like position at the end of the backswing and a curtailed loop is to return to the delayed toss as on the beginner's serve.

While we are working out these details, however, we must keep the whole swing in mind—a synchronized, free-flowing, continuous-action swing based on balance and rhythm. A swing that enables the racket to reach its maximum speed at point of impact is our goal. It is important, always, to develop a simple swing without hitches and body contortions that allows the racket to flow smoothly and gather speed as it comes in.

There is a final challenge for the instructor: how to convince his pupil that the serve cannot be developed through instruction and playing *alone*; that it is, in fact, developed (in the final analysis) *by regular and dedicated practice*—by the pupil with a basket of balls working for hours on his particular problems.

VARIETY IN THE GROUNDSTROKES

Flexibility is the key word for the groundstrokes now. Depending on how a player has developed, this may be a period for consolidation of control over topspin and underspin, power and finesse; it may also be a period of augmentation. If a player's strength has been a topspin forehand, he may need to add more underspin shots; if it has been an underspin backhand, then he will want to work on topspin. Any player can go a long way with one kind of forehand and one kind of backhand, but the ideal is to have a variety of shots.

Once we looked at spin as something to break up an opponent's game (and it can still be considered important against some players on clay); now its importance is in defense against the Big Game. If the way for a player to defense the Big Game is through finesse, then a varied assortment of stroke equipment is necessary. This is the goal: command of both spins on both sides. Flexibility is always one of my main concerns.

Often, on this level, we work with players who have forehand problems (not our pupils, of course!). I call this "forehand-itis," and I have a few pet theories about it. The problem can arise out of the way a forehand has been taught, of course—the left foot crosses the right, etc.—but I feel that there is a psychological factor in it also. The forehand is supposed to be the great shot, you know. There is a strong theory in tennis that backhands shouldn't be hit, just kept in play—perhaps never more than sliced, and never hit anywhere but into the other fellow's backhand—then the ball comes to your forehand (provided of course, that your opponent is not a follower of this theory) and Pow! The point is over. Good theory. I like it. But I've got a little thing going that says this has contributed somewhat to forehand-itis. Let me quote a lesson to show you what I mean.

This pupil was an advanced player who played the lesser circuits and was ranked well up in his Section. Properly certified. But, he told me, he had forehand trouble.

I hit a variety of balls to his backhand. Very nice. He hit the short ones with a good chip shot and came in. He drove the waist-high balls deep and cross-court with a sound flat stroke. When he was wide, he would automatically slice a slow deep ball to give himself time to get back into position. Rather flexible here, I thought. He always sliced the high balls and skipped nicely for fairly close ones.

And then it happened! I hit one to his forehand. Up cocked the wrist; out stiffened the arm, and he started a frantic run for the ball, ending with the left foot well across the right. Pow, the big forehand hit the fence. He never varied this pattern once on his forehand side, no matter where I hit the ball, but always made a big attempt to get underneath the ball and to cover it—to make the great forehand shot. He did mix his shots in one way— by hitting into the net and into the fence. Every now and then, however, the shot would go in, and he seemed a little perplexed when it did.

I called him up to the net and said, "That's a pretty good backhand you have there."

"I know, Pro, but what about this forehand?"

"Well," I said, "tell me something. You rather enjoy slicing your back-hand; you used it on at least three playing situations, but you never use under-spin on your forehand. Why?"

His look told me everything. It said, "I'm not supposed to; this is my *big shot.*"

"All right," I said, "Now I want you to hit a few forehands with underspin. I want you to forget that this right side must be some letter-perfect flat or topspin shot out of the books. One of your problems is that you don't match the bounce of the ball correctly at the end of the backswing. Much of the time you are too far below the ball when you start your forward swing. When this is true, it's often easier to control the ball by coming down into it. Now forget for a moment that you have to apply topspin to the ball; let's see what a little underspin will do for you. I want you to come down into a few forehands."

There was a minor struggle for a time, but soon the ball started reaching the baseline with a nice trajectory over the net and good depth (he had a lot of ability). He ended the lesson not with a new forehand but with a new shot in which he had considerably more confidence than he had in his rigid application of the great forehand.

At the end of the lesson, I explained to him that he should use this kind of action on the ball when he was returning the hard serve, when he was wide and coming-in, and whenever he was off balance. I explained that this would help him to relax on his forehand side and get that one more ball into court. I told him to use it whenever forehand-itis bothered him.

Now I don't mean to indicate that this is the final solution to forehand-itis. In the above lesson, I made *no corrections* of the poor forehand. If we had had the time, we would have talked about staying away from the ball. I would have suggested skip steps, because when the ball is approached on the forehand side with the right foot as a measure or index of distance, most players gain a new sense of judging distance.

Had we had the time, we would have talked about watching the ball. It is my contention that on a strong side, players watch the ball more care-fully. They can do more with the ball, shade it, place it more accurately, and so they watch it intensely. On the weak side, players seem to feel that they can't hit the thing, so they don't really watch it.

Open Footwork on the Forehand.

We would also have talked about tension, which goes with every bad forehand. I was, of course, making the first dent with my suggestion that he use under-the-ball action to gain the flexibility I saw in his backhand.

Too, we would have discussed the business of ball control (as outlined in Part II of this book. Yes, we'd need to go back that far!). One of the basic causes of forehand-itis is the feeling of having to apply topspin to the ball mechanically by turning the racket over the ball, or starting too far below it and brushing it.

Earlier timing, more rotation, and more right shoulder in the shot would be three other areas of importance, but we would constantly work on the footwork problem, making certain that the player hit with a straight or open stance, always trying to keep the left foot out of the way. That left foot—"It's a bag of cement," Wayne Sabin says.

But our initial concept (in this lesson) would not change; there is nothing in the rule book that disqualifies underspin in the shape of the stroke, on either backhand or forehand side.

B. Improvisation

One of the hallmarks of the advanced player is the "educated wrist." It can be most important: a way to get deception; a way to recoup when the ball is mistimed; a way to handle bad bounces. It is most valuable on the low volley. Good wrist action is one of the ways an advanced player will improvise to meet the many problems caused by the increased tempo of advanced tennis. In short, it will add to the flexibility of your player's stroke production.

We have taught open footwork on the forehand side for wide shots and approach shots and on the backhand for approach shots *only*. Now it will be used on return of serve, on both backhand and forehand when it is impossible to use a straight stance because of the time element. Open footwork will occur more and more frequently on this level of play, as adjustments must be made to the increased tempo.

A. Using the Whole Court

Before the player is ready for pressure tennis, there are a few more steps to be taken. During this period, we will be stressing some of Chet Murphy's "play situations" tactics. Further let me say that Wayne Sabin's patterned, cross-court, waiting-for-the-short-ball player is my kind of player too. In addition, I like two other kinds of player. To consider one of them, let's hark back to "Tennis—Past and Present," to that small glimpse of baseline tennis as played inside the baseline by Williams and Cochet. This is the ultimate in what I will refer to as "the whole court" game—*the ability to attack all of an opponent's court from the baseline.* (We've seen an approximation of it recently in the game of Rosewall.)

The "whole court idea" concerns choice of shots and presents a more elaborate pattern than we have worked on so far.

Choice of shots is based on the following factors:

1. what a player can do (the kinds of shots he can make)
2. his position in the court
3. his opponent's position in the court, and
4. his opponent's weakness

Of course, choice is always modified by the court surface. The player's position in court is on or just behind the baseline.

What a player *can* do should always rule his decisions. Once he is grooved in a sound pattern of *deep* cross-court hitting on the backhand side, I want him to work on the cross-court angled shot. In my opinion, the ability to do this well is not accomplished until early in the advanced stage. My next step is to encourage the down-the-line shot, but only on balls that have not been hit into the corners, but rather closer to the center of court. I want my pupil to be able to hit this shot into his opponent's forehand corner. As he gets better at this, I encourage him to use the straight backhand shot when he

20 | CHOICE OF SHOTS

must hit from closer to the line, say, after he has used the short cross-court backhand and his opponent is out of position. These shots can be used off cross-court shots from the opponent or off straight shots. Both can have the effect of putting the opponent off balance. The latter is called a "cross-up" play.

We can apply this pattern of development to the forehand also. It is important to be able to hit the angle here, and the straight shot, and I want him to be able to move around the centered balls and hit on his forehand, deep to the backhand corner, or to angle it.

When these straight shots are made with plenty of time for the player to return to position, they can have the effect of "opening up the opponent's court" for the next shot. This is particularly true on the fast surfaces, and the straight backhand is particularly important for breaking up a cross-court pattern player's game. To play this whole court game means, of course, that our player is hitting the ball earlier. It is his taking an early ball that prevents an opponent from getting back into position ("the matter of inches that can make the difference," as Van Horn puts it). It has given us the opportunity to use the angles, to hit with more speed and to get to the net.

It should be added that the short cross-court angle shots must be good enough to keep an opponent outside the sidelines. As Bill Lufler says, "if we can keep a man behind or outside the lines, we can't get hurt."

All of this work is building a player who can play *with imagination*. He knows that there is often *more than one shot* for a given situation. He won't do it all with speed; a soft short ball or a soft sharp angle when he is playing on clay may set the scene for an offensive lob or an easy passing shot as his opponent reaches the net, off balance.

Yes, he's my kind of player, too!

Perhaps, like Rosewall, he'll add more all-out attack later, and then he'll use the whole court from the net, angles into the short corners from both sides and the short straight volleys as well as the stop volleys.

We have brought our player now up to the point where he can think of a *sequence of shots*; in the following piece, Dennis Van der Meer notes this principle.

Oh, yes,—that third type of player; he plays the Big Game! He backs it up, of course, with *sound defense*. Perhaps he'll be able to play all three types of game and shift from one to the other when he's losing.

B. Units of Play

(*Dennis Van der Meer*)

Quite often, when I'm teaching an intermediate, I may suddenly belt a serve. He will always express awe and say, "How does anyone hit a ball like that back?" Sometimes, he will comment on fast reactions on a first exchange of volleys he has seen by good doubles players.

I explain that the good player returns the serve that I have just hit with comparative ease because he knows in advance *what is going to happen from the moment the ball leaves his racket.* The "computer" in his brain, which has been built through years of experience, tells him that that ball is going to be whizzing toward him in the next fraction of a second and is going to rebound in a recognizable way, and that he had better start correlating his movements and his knowledge to this approaching ball.

The same principle applies when, in a quick exchange of volleys in doubles, a player suddenly moves to the center of the court and cuts off a volley. His "computer," recognizing the playing situation, has told him that the ball is going to go down the center.

The increasing ability to recognize the game in terms of "units of strokes" rather than individual strokes is a very important step in a player's gradual development.

Let's take this unit of play: my opponent hits me a short cross-court forehand drive. I play an approach shot down the line. He tries to pass me with a cross-court backhand drive, and I finish the point with a straight backhand volley. This is a recognizable *playing unit.* There are two other recognizable situations here: the opponent could try to pass me down the line, in which case I would play a cross-court angled forehand volley, or he could lob, in which case I would hit an overhead to a predetermined spot.

The point to stress is that there should be no question marks in the player's mind. He has seen a given playing sequence so many times that there should be no hesitation in his dispatch of the ball.

C. The Right Shot at The Right Time

(Chet Murphy)

In first-class competitive tennis as it is played today, the winning player is usually the one who makes most effective use of his serve and his volleys. Ranking players depend so heavily on these shots that the serve, which is usually used as a preparatory shot for a volley, is called "the biggest single weapon in modern tennis."

This is true, however, only in matches played on the fast grass courts of the Eastern Circuit and on the hard courts found in the West. There, ground-strokes are usually used only as supplementary strokes, but in matches played on slower surfaces, such as clay and composition, even "first ten" players often decide against using aggressive net-rushing tactics. They often depend, instead, on accurate steady baseline play.

Contrary to what many inexperienced players believe, successful backcourt play is not simply a matter of hitting the ball back more often than does the opponent. True, we often see or hear of "dinkers" or "pushers" who depend on steadiness and retrieving ability alone to win. But many baseliners who stroke soundly and steadily, who are masters of position play and use superior tactics to draw errors from their opponents, are often unjustly accused of being "pushers." Actually, however, many of them could be described more accurately as "cagey baseliners." For they understand and appreciate fully that in tennis, as in boxing, aggressiveness by itself is not the formula for winning. Indeed, aggressiveness may sometimes be foolhardy. A smart baseliner, by skillful intelligent application of a few basic principles, can do much to lessen the effectiveness of an aggressive opponent's attack.

Let us present and discuss here a few of the guiding principles used successfully by baseline players in both topflight tournament play and, at a lower level, club play.

Perhaps the most outstanding quality such players have is the ability to make, or at least to select, the right shot at the right time. Through study and experience, they know immediately which shot offers the best opportunity for them to keep the ball in play and to get out of trouble, or to force the opponent into trying a difficult shot, or to lure him into a dangerous position. By combining defensive and aggressive shots and by applying sound principles of position play, they succeed in prolonging rallies so that they can wait until the right time to become the aggressor, and they often succeed in luring their opponents into trying to end rallies too soon. In other words, they make their opponents play badly. Only when the opponents restrain their own impulsive, aggressive tendencies and temper their games to match the sound baseliner in steadiness, accuracy, and craftiness are the baseliners in danger of losing. And then, when they lose, it is usually only to better players equipped with as much knowledge of tactics and strategy as they and with even more ability to stroke the ball and to move around the court.

Learning to select the right shot at the right time may be simplified by classifying the possibilities as follows; in a match, every shot ought to be hit for one of the following reasons:

(1) as a defensive shot
(2) to keep the ball in play (when that alone will be adequate)
(3) to secure good position
(4) to move an opponent
(5) to set up a kill, or
(6) to make a kill

Reasons 1, 2, and 3 are used in a match in conjunction with the basic position play that we have already discussed.

Though many players are familiar with position play, and apply it when playing at the net, few of them understand how to apply it in baseline play. They seem to be unaware of the fact that when playing from the backcourt, in order to be in position on the line that bisects, they will oftentimes have to move in a direction *opposite* from that in which their opponent has moved to play his shot. Probably the reason they fail to apply this principle in baseline play is that they hear so often that a player should always return to a spot midway between his sidelines after making a return. Actually, this is not true, and it is not done by experienced tournament players. The only time a baseliner should return to the center of his baseline, or to a spot precisely behind his center marker, is when the opponent is hitting from the center of *his* baseline, or from a spot very close to the center. Only then will the line that bisects, drawn from the opponent's position, be midway between the sidelines as it crosses the opposite baseline. At all other times, this line that bisects will be either to the right or left of the center mark, depending on the opponent's hitting position.

In order to play the right shot at the right time, a baseliner must be able to control the *depth* of his shots. He must be able to hit deep when he wants to, and short when necessary. A pupil who does this understands the concept of "hitting into levels."

To summarize: it can be said that players who do not possess quick reactions, strong serves, and other special skills and qualities necessary for successful net play may be wiser to develop steady, accurate, consistent groundstrokes and to rely on these groundstrokes, together with sound tactics and strategy, to win. Sound tactics simply means being in the right place at the right time and making the right shot at the right time—making the opponent use strokes he doesn't like and make the kind of shots he doesn't like, from places in the court he doesn't like.

Sound tactics means knowing your own strengths and weaknesses and using your strength in match play. It means knowing or discovering your opponent's strengths and weaknesses, covering his strong shots and forcing him to play his weak ones. It means probing for weaknesses and analyzing the trend of the match, so that a player can continue to apply tactics if they are winning for him and yet be prepared to change if the opponent has countered with successful new tactics. Even though much time has been spent on developing his strokes, a player must always remember that strokes will be of little value to him unless he knows how and when to use them to win a point.

(Wayne Sabin)

The basic ABC tactics of the great players are to be steady and deep off the ground until you get the short ball—then apply the great principle: make your approach and make your first volley and you have to win your match.

Of course, you stick around and play the second or third volley, or smash, or whatever. The implication is that if you will make your approach and make your first volley, this accomplishment alone is enough to tip the scales in your favor.

Truly excellent tennis is not a game of wild, hard-hitting, erratic shots. Excellent tennis is an exhibition of beautifully poised skill that has been accumulated through years of concentrated effort and discipline. Tilden rightly stated that it takes five years to make a tennis player and ten years to make a champion—that means five to ten years of devoted endeavor and discipline.

No discussion of tennis tactics is complete without bringing up the name of Frankie Parker; certainly a young aspirant's grasp of tactics can be broadened by a close examination of this remarkable man's tennis. What a case history is Parker! No man showed more conclusively that tennis is, indeed, a game of skill.

A check of the records will show that from 1933 through 1949, for seventeen consecutive years, Parker was ranked among the first ten players in the country. Thirteen of those years he was ranked among the first five, and twice he won Forest Hills, the National Championship, and was ranked No. 1. I think you'll agree that's quite an impressive record, but what is even more impressive is how he did it.

A man may be born with ability, but no man is born with skill. Skill is a human cultivation, and if Parker was born short of one, he was, indeed, long on the cultivation of the other.

In all the years I played against Parker and watched him play, I never saw him hit a hard ball. Parker did not have the

TACTICS OF
THE GREAT

21

physical makeup to hit hard. He had a lifetime quarrel with a balky forehand. He never served an ace. His backhand, although amazingly controlled, was hit quite modestly. No one ever commented on the merits of his net game. He did not have quick reflexes. He could not run very fast, or jump very high. He never lunged for a volley 18 inches beyond his reach. Parker took this mediocre equipment and this commonplace ability and carved out his remarkable record.

If this is an accurate description of Parker (and it is), then how could such a run-of-the-mill athlete establish such a record? You guessed it—tactics. Frank Parker was "Mr. Tactics" himself.

First off, Parker recognized and accepted his own limitations and never tried to play beyond them. Second, Parker was keenly aware that *matches are lost—not won—it is always the player with the fewer errors who wins.* So Parker undertook the exacting discipline of ball control. He worked hard and for years to become as errorless as humanly possible and left it to his opponents to try to do something with the ball.

Parker's serve was simply the method by which the ball was put into play. Once the ball was in play, the contest began—and just what was that contest? Parker's total effort was to hit the ball firmly to within 6 or 8 feet of his opponent's baseline—cross-court, leaving Parker in the center of the playing court for his opponent's return. If his opponent had a weaker side, Parker kept the ball deep and steadily into that weaker side. Remember, Parker had worked for years to develop air-tight control off the ground and he proved what he suspected, that no man could get the ball out of his reach by any combination of power hits, as long as Parker could keep his man behind the baseline with depth—that the greatest volleyer could not successfully hit from behind the baseline and come to the net against him—that no net-rushing server could prevail against the pinpoint accuracy of his return of serve. Parker knew that if he could pin his opponent to the baseline with depth, regardless of his opponent's strength and power-hitting, that unless his opponent could match the skill of Parker's depth and steadiness, his opponent was more likely to err first, or to yield the *first short ball.*

When Parker got the short ball, again with depth, he would firmly hit his approach to his opponent's weaker side, or down the middle to give his opponent a minimum target, and with physical and mental poise Parker took up his position at the net, three or four feet inside the service line, and let his opponent try to pass him from behind the baseline. Parker proved that the greatest ground games in the world could not pass him enough to win. As long as he kept his volley firm and deep into his opponent's weaker side, or firm and deep down the middle, Parker had to end up with the winning margin of points. And mind you, Parker was only an adequate volleyer, nothing outstanding.

Parker played the ABC's of tactics to perfection. If Parker was not a great player with this blueprint, he certainly was the test of a great player. He separated the cream from the milk, and it was, indeed, a sight to behold to watch the power players of his era (Kovacs, **Kramer**, McNeill, Schroeder, etc.) pound their brains out against the impenetrable wall of Parker's defense. There were two ways you could not beat Parker. You could not blast him off the court, and you could not very well out-steady him. The only way to beat Parker was with the Master Blueprint itself. You had to be able to stay with Parker from the baseline until you got the short ball, and then—*make* your approach, and *make* your first volley, and you had to win your match. To beat Parker you had to be a great player.

This, too, is the way the great players have played the game, modifying it with their own strengths and weaknesses, their own idiosyncrasies, temperaments and individual abilities.

Take Tilden—he played this way from the baseline, but because he was not good at the net, he hesitated to go there; he preferred to take the short ball and put it away with his great forehand.

After Tilden came Vines. Vines played tennis a great deal the way Tilden did, with great groundstrokes and a tremendous forehand, but he was more effective at the net than Tilden, and he was one of the great smashers and servers of all time. He swept the world. Still, he was not a great volleyer, but he was extremely strong from the baseline, particularly on the forehand; and he would force you and shatter you out of what you thought was airtight baseline control. It was hard to hold Vines or Tilden down from the baseline because their force was so great that they broke you up; then you would give them the short ball.

Fred Perry played the game perfectly. He came after Vines, with airtight baseline play and a fine maneuvering forehand. When he got the short ball, in to the net he went. He made his approach; he made his first volley; he put you out of position.

After Perry came Budge, the same type of player. He had a great ground game—greater even than the other three . . . the greatest ground game of all time, perhaps, with airtight strength and steadiness from the baseline. He would increase his speed until you "had a machine against you," hitting the ball twice as hard as you were. He wouldn't miss, with every ball hit coming in within three or four feet of the baseline. What could you do? If you came in to the net, your head would get knocked off; you wouldn't get inside the service line, and you couldn't stay at the baseline. He was a great baseline player.

After Budge came Riggs, a great court general. He played the game with an airtight baseline.

Then came Kramer, who changed the rules a bit. Jack capitalized on some tremendous strengths—a great serve, volley, and forehand—and added one new ingredient, the importance of *getting to the net*, whether serving or receiving. He called it the Big Game. He kept the pressure on; he kept doing it and doing it, until his opponent got tired of threading needles to pass him. He was extremely effective in this innovation, playing singles the way great doubles are played.

After Kramer came Gonzales, who was one of the great attackers of all time but a steady defender, also. He didn't try to do anything until he got the short ball, and then he was in, like a cat. Of course, his serve was his greatest weapon; this man changed the basic tactics only according to this strength.

After Gonzales: Sedgeman, one of the great body handlers of all time. Others were Perry and Gonzales. They handled their bodies as if they weighed fifteen pounds, and as if there was nothing to flying all over the court. Sedgeman was not a steady player from the baseline; he lingered as little as possible on the baseline and came in at the earliest possible chance. A fine volleyer, he used this strength to the utmost.

Finally, Hoad and Rosewall. Hoad had a lot of talent; he served and went in to the net fast. Rosewall's was the last of the great ground games, and if you check the records you will see that he stopped Hoad cold in the big ones. Rosewall was a great player because of his ground game and his ability to supplement it with excellent net play.

So this is how the great players, from Tilden to Rosewall, used these basic tactics but adapted them to their own abilities. The men who had the great ground games—Tilden, Budge, Riggs, Perry—devoted a great deal of time to this phase of the game.

We, as coaches, must keep in mind that the whole game should be developed from, and that basic tactics begin with, sound defense of the baseline. In order to learn sound defense, a player must devote considerable time to developing sound shots off both sides. This is orthodox, the very heart of the ABC's of tactics. Without the ABC's, we cannot play airtight, steady tennis from the baseline, setting the scene for the short ball, deep approach, and deep volley.

The Ground Game

Off the ground, as everywhere else, the finished player makes the game look easy. His strokes may not be classic, but sound action in the hitting area provides control of the ball. Always, the racket does the work. The player's footwork is agile and varied. He has balance, but if sometimes he is caught off balance and has to improvise, he finds that the years of training have conditioned his muscles to react automatically; he will be on balance in an off-balance position. He has rhythm.

He can hit with depth and speed into the corners, but he can make the sharp angles, too. In short, he uses the whole court of his opponent. He has developed a very special tool—the educated wrist. He uses it to get deception and, under special circumstances, for ball control and placement.

He has more than one stroke on each side. He adjusts the size of each stroke to the job at hand, very possibly to the court surface. He has the flat shots to the openings for placements or straight passing shots, the short topspin shots and delicate chips to keep the ball low.

The Serve

The finished player recognizes the value of the serve as an offensive weapon, and he uses all the serves—slice, flat, overspin, and American Twist—depending on his opponent's weakness and the court surface: a slice to the backhand in the left court to keep his opponent from running around his forehand; an American Twist to his backhand in this court to pull him out of court; a slice to the forehand in the right court for the same effect; a slice to the forehand in the left court and an American Twist to the backhand in the right to keep

THE FINISHED
PLAYER

22

his opponent in the center of court and to cut down his angles. Occasionally, he will serve straight at his man if the situation demands it. In all of this, he will have deception; he keeps his opponent guessing.

He averages about 70 per cent of his first serves. Usually this serve is hit at about three-quarters speed. He serves the big cannonball for the big points. He takes time between his first and his second serve, which he hits deep, generally to the backhand, with more spin than the first.

He comes in behind his serve on the fast surfaces, but he is smart enough to know that against a good return of serve he cannot do this consistently on clay. He always covers his opponent's best shots.

He may use a long flowing swing or a shorter one, but whichever he uses there is a rhythm and precision about his serve that gives him consistency.

Coming in to the Net

This player keeps the ball deep and plays it for position or weakness. He will also utilize the center-of-court theory. He may have one method, underspin action, or he may combine this with flat and topspin hitting, depending on the height of the ball. He runs through this shot and knows the importance of moving fast into position once he has made it. He always comes to a split stop just before his opponent hits the ball. He knows that he must never miss this shot (he knows, of course, that he must never miss the easy shots anywhere—approaches, volleys, or groundstrokes), but there's a special green light shining on this one. He will at times use the drop shot because he knows that the more shots his opponent must worry about, the more effective he will be.

His technique will be a short swing—short in the backswing because he is running through the ball and this will give him the necessary speed of shot; short in the follow-through because he must be able to run, to volley.

If he comes in from farther back than usual, he will hit the ball slowly, high and deep with considerable spin, to give him the time to get in to the net.

The Volley

The finished player is never careless at the net. He has a Midas touch here. He has the ability to anticipate, the agility to cut off the passing shots. He knows there are different sizes of volley stroke, and he uses the compact punch or jab on the tough fast balls, a half swing volley on the slower ones. He has the speed and pace on the high balls to score winners, control and touch on his low volleys.

Usually his first volley will be deep unless he has the angle to make an immediate placement. He will place the ball to a weakness or use the straight volley for position play. Often he will utilize the center-of-court theory to keep his opponent's angles down.

He knows his opponent's best passing shots and will always have them covered, but often he will fake an opening and close in fast when his opponent tries to take advantage of it.

Return of Serve

The finished player knows the importance of being consistent in serving. He does not always go for a winner; rather, he has control over the short low shots and can place them at will, cross-court, down the line, or right at his opponent's feet. Occasionally, he will rock the net rusher with chips and lobs.

If his opponent stays back, he can hit the ball deep and is always ready to pounce on a weak shot to take the offensive away from the server. When the serve is too fast for average stroking, he can rely on a short block or a chip, to get the ball back into court. He will vary his position and his type of return until he has found the solution to breaking serve.

Strategy and Tactics

This player uses his strengths to pattern his style of play. He has an over-all plan for winning mapped out at the start of every match, but he realizes that often the tactics to carry out this plan must be changed as his opponent finds answers to them. He will change his over-all plan as quickly as he will his tactics, if it is necessary. He will always change a losing game; just as surely, he will never change a winning one. Above all, his defense is just as much an art as his attacking game. He can use the defensive lob, the slow high shot when out of position, and he can mix topspin and chip shots with offensive lobs. He will often play the ball to be in position for using his best shot against his opponent's second best. He fully understands the importance of position play but will temper position play to exploit weaknesses.

Match Play

The finished player is a study in concentration. Changing courts may give him a moment of relaxation in which to think about his mistakes and his opponent's weaknesses and to consider whether he is in need of a strategical or tactical change of play, but his mind never wanders from those four lines, his opponent, and the ball.

He has tenacity and patience, and he knows the court is a battlefield. He's a fighter, and every move he makes is toward winning. He knows that winning tennis is a state of mind, that in the final analysis, all things being equal, matches are won with the heart and the head. He may play continually fired-up or with cold composure, but either way he has a dread of defeat.

He has complete self-control. He knows that linesmen can make bad calls and that he will get some of them. He knows that he will make bad shots, but he never lingers over them; each one is forgotten with the next point. He is composed and confident at all times.

He has a mysterious quality that enables him to come through on the big points. He uses gutsmanship instead of gamesmanship with no question in his mind about who is master.

Pauline Betz Addie

One of the all-time greats in women's tennis, she was ranked among the top ten players for seven years and was national champion in 1942, 1943, 1944 and 1946. After becoming Wimbledon champion in 1946, she turned professional in 1947 and was undefeated in professional tournaments or tours until 1961. She is married to Bob Addie, Washington sports columnist. A teaching professional in the Washington area, she is currently running a summer tennis camp at Sidwell Friends School, Washington, D. C. She is the author of *Tennis For Teen Agers*.

Bill Lufler

For thirty-five years, Lufler has been an outstanding college coach and club professional. His college coaching at Presbyterian College in Clinton, South Carolina and at the University of Miami brought him national fame. A tennis internationalist, he worked for the Swedish Lawn Tennis Association for six years as National Coach.

As a player he was a member of the William T. Tilden tours in 1938 and in 1946-47. He was ranked fifth among the American professionals in 1948.

He has been president of the Professional Lawn Tennis Association and is currently its Executive Director. For the past seven years he has been professional at the West Side Tennis Club in Forest Hills, New York.

ABOUT
THE CONTRIBUTORS

Bill Murphy

He has been tennis coach at the University of Michigan since 1948. His teams have won one National Collegiate championship and nine Big Ten championships. In dual matches, their record is 190-28. He is a past president of the National Collegiate Tennis Coaches Association and the Big Ten Coaches Association, and a past chairman of the National Collegiate Athletic Association Tennis Committee. He is a member of the USLTA Junior Development committee and the Lifetime Sports Foundation tennis staff. With his brother, he is co-author of two books on the game, *Tennis Handbook* and *Tennis For Beginners*.

Chet Murphy

As a player, Murphy won the Big Ten championships in Singles and Doubles, and was a finalist one year in the National Collegiate Singles and Doubles.

Past president of the National Collegiate Tennis Association, Murphy was also a tennis coach at the Universities of Chicago, Detroit and Minnesota before becoming coach at the University of California. Since then his U. C. teams have finished third twice, and fifth twice in NCAA play. One of the foremost "teachers of teachers" in the country, he has conducted workshops for teachers for the Lifetime Sports Foundation of the AAHPER. He holds a doctorate in education from the University of Michigan.

Wayne Sabin

From 1935 to 1949, Sabin was one of the top figures in the world of tournament tennis. For several years as an amateur and later as a touring professional, he established himself as one of the game's great competitors, with victories in major competition over such all-time greats as Tilden, Riggs, Budge, Kramer, and Perry. He was a member of the U. S. Davis Cup team and winner of many major tournaments.

Always a student of the game, with a keen sense of analysis and interpretation, Sabin stepped naturally into the field of teaching, and for the past two decades has established himself as one of the outstanding teachers of tennis. He is also the owner-operator of the Wayne Sabin Tennis Camp, which has attracted hundreds of young aspirants from all over the world.

Dennis Van der Meer

A leading amateur player in South Africa, Van der Meer turned professional at the age of 20, and became the first president of the South African Professional Tennis Association. He has been professional at the Berkeley Tennis Club, Berkeley, California, for the past eight years, where his record in Junior development has been outstanding. Many of his pupils have won national titles. A highly imaginative instructor, he is much in demand as a teacher of tennis teachers at various clinics. He also runs a very successful summer tennis camp. He is married to the former Linda Vail, Intercollegiate Girls' champion of 1960.

Welby Van Horn

As an amateur player, Van Horn was the youngest player to reach the final round of the National Men's Singles Championships at Forest Hills—a record he still holds. Two years later he turned professional and proceeded to prove himself one of the great players of his time, with wins over Fred Perry, Wayne Sabin, Frank Kovacs, Bobby Riggs, and others.

Welby's fame, however, rests on his achievements as a teaching professional at the Caribe Hilton in Puerto Rico. Through 1965, twenty-one students have received 94 U. S. National rankings; six have won 18 National Championships. Welby is that rare exception in the teaching business—a great player who went on to become a great teacher.

INDEX